Attachment Play

Attachment Play

How to solve children's behavior problems
with play, laughter, and connection

Aletha J. Solter, PH.D.

SHINING STAR PRESS ✶ GOLETA, CALIFORNIA

Published by Shining Star Press
Post Office Box 206
Goleta, California 93116, U.S.A.
Phone & Fax: (805) 968–1868

Email: info@awareparenting.com
Website: www.awareparenting.com (The Aware Parenting Institute)

Book design: Studio E Books, Santa Barbara

Cover photo by Michael Rose, New South Wales, Australia
www.taodesigns.com.au

First printing 2013

Publisher's Cataloging Information
Solter, Aletha Jauch, 1945–
Attachment play: how to solve children's behavior problems with play, laughter,
and connection / by Aletha J. Solter
Includes bibliographical references.
ISBN: 978-0-9613073-8-7
1. Child rearing. 2. Parent and child. 3. Psychology of play. I. Title.
Dewey Decimal Classification: 649'.1

Library of Congress Control Number: 2012948709

I tried to teach my child with books.
He gave me only puzzled looks.
I used clear words to discipline,
But I never seemed to win.
Despairingly, I turned aside.
"How shall I reach this child?" I cried.
Into my hand he put the key:
"Come," he said, "Play with me."

—Author unknown
(adapted by Aletha Solter)

Acknowledgments

I would like to thank everybody who read the manuscript and gave helpful feedback. My main editors were my husband, Ken Solter, my son, Nicholas Solter, and my daughter-in-law, Sonja Solter. Additional readers who provided useful feedback were Dr. Maria Fisk, Melanie Jacobson, Stephanie Jamgochian, and Heather Stevenson.

I would also like to thank all the parents (in several countries) who contributed play examples for this book. Their anecdotes serve to illustrate and clarify the concepts. All names have been changed except for those of my own children. I am also grateful to all the parents who have consulted with me, because I have learned something new from each consultation.

Finally, I would like to acknowledge my colleague, Dr. Mary Galbraith, who first coined the term "attachment play."

Contents

Appendix A

Appendix B

Warning/Disclaimer

As an educational resource for parents, this book offers suggestions for helpful ways to play with your child. These suggestions may not be appropriate for children suffering from certain physical, emotional, or behavioral problems. This book is not intended to replace psychotherapy or medical help from competent professionals. If your child is suffering from physical, emotional, or behavioral problems, it is recommended that you obtain professional advice and treatment.

The mention of specific therapies in this book is for informational purposes only and does not entail endorsement by the author. Some forms of therapy can be dangerous if carried out by improperly trained practitioners. If you are considering choosing a therapist for yourself or your child, it is important to carefully review the therapist's credentials and references.

Some traumas can overwhelm children and families, and the suggestions in this book may be inappropriate or insufficient to help children heal, especially in cases of physical or sexual abuse, neglect, medical trauma, the death of a family member, natural disasters, and terrorism or war.

The author and publisher offer no guarantee for the effectiveness of the suggestions in this book, and they shall have neither liability nor responsibility to any person or entity with respect to any damage caused, or alleged to be caused, directly or indirectly by the information contained in this book.

Attachment Play

Introduction

DID YOU KNOW that discipline doesn't always have to be serious, stressful, tedious, or frustrating and that you can solve many of your children's behavior problems with certain kinds of playful activities? That's what this book is all about. Maybe you don't want to use a punitive approach but are at a loss to know how to change your children's behavior. Or perhaps you vacillate between an authoritarian approach and an overly permissive one, wondering how to find a middle ground.

This book will describe playful activities that can reduce stress, strengthen attachment, and solve behavior problems while bringing laughter and joy to you and your children. Whether you have a toddler or a pre-teen, you will be delighted to discover how easy it can be to change your child's behavior without the use of punishment. Through specific kinds of playful activities, you can "win" your children over and resolve discipline problems, sometimes quite effortlessly. The approach to discipline described in the book is neither authoritarian nor permissive. You will learn how to set necessary limits in ways that inspire your children to cooperate rather than rebel.

The book delves beneath the surface of typical discipline problems by addressing some of the sources of stress that lie at the root of challenging behaviors. Your children's behavior may become more difficult when they are stressed by factors such as the birth of a sibling, medical procedures, or school. The play-based suggestions in the book will empower you with tools to help your children through these difficult times. As your children work through these stresses and release tensions, their behavior will improve.

The theoretical rationale for this book is attachment theory. In the 1950's, the famous British doctor and psychoanalyst, John Bowlby, first used the term *attachment* to refer to a child's bond with his parents. Since then, a large body of knowledge has accumulated about the importance of parent-child attachment. Social interaction, beginning in infancy, is at the root of healthy attachment. When children lack a responsive, joyful relationship with their parents, or when they have been traumatized in some way, their attachment weakens, and this can lead to a host of behavioral and emotional problems.

During the past 25 years, I have developed a unique synthesis of highly effective and enjoyable parent-child play activities, which I call *attachment play*. These activities are supported by research in the fields of attachment, therapy, and neuroscience.

Did you know that positive social interaction stimulates the production of oxytocin, a "feel-good" chemical that reduces stress and promotes growth and healing while enhancing your children's brain development? Cooperative play stimulates areas of the brain involved in the control of aggressive behavior, and laughter resolves anger and anxiety by reducing stress hormones. Following traumatic experiences, you can literally "rewire" your children's brains through specific kinds of play that help them recover from trauma.

I have found that these activities work well with children of all ages and with families of many different cultures. Parents around the world are often amazed at the beneficial changes they see in their children after engaging them in these unique forms of play.

Attachment play has several distinctive characteristics, which differentiate it from traditional games or sports. It is child centered, often involves laughter, does not require any special equipment, and it can take place anywhere, at any time. In addition, it is non-competitive and has no set rules.

Children love attachment play and often initiate it. In fact, you may already be practicing some forms of attachment play but may not realize the deeper significance or usefulness of these activities. This book will explain the deeper meaning of these familiar activities (such as the game of hide-and-seek). It will also describe the value of engaging children in these forms of play to resolve specific kinds of conflicts. Sometimes children's invitations to play take the form of annoying behaviors, which you may interpret as silliness, rudeness, or a waste of time. This book will help you interpret these behaviors differently and respond in ways that foster connection and cooperation.

I structured the book around typical discipline issues as well as specific sources of stress, so each chapter can stand on its own. You can therefore easily find relevant information and practical suggestions for your particular family situation without having to read the entire book. However, reading the whole book is useful because you might discover underlying reasons for your children's behavior that you had not considered.

To illustrate the various forms of play, I have included numerous real-life examples from interviews with parents and from my experience as a consultant, parent-child play coach, workshop leader, mother, and grandmother. I hope that these examples and anecdotes will inspire and entertain you and that you will be eager to try attachment play with your own children.

The age range of the book is from birth to age twelve. Most of the techniques can be adapted to different ages even though the specific examples that inspire you might describe children that are younger (or older) than yours.

My wish for all parents is that you will enjoy many moments of playful connection with your children. Are you ready for the giggles?

Organization of the book

In Part 1 (Getting Started), you will find a description of nine basic forms of attachment play as well as some guidelines for getting started with this approach. I recommend reading all of this section because the rest of the book is based on it. Furthermore, it will provide you with ideas for immediate, concrete activities that you can try with your children. The last chapter in this section explores some of the barriers you might have to playing with your children, and it includes a series of personal exercises to explore these difficulties.

Part 2 (Using Attachment Play to Solve Discipline Problems) describes a complete, play-based approach to non-punitive discipline, organized according to typical behavior problems. Each chapter describes a variety of playful approaches for resolving that specific conflict. These approaches are based on the nine forms of play described in Part 1.

Part 3 (Using Attachment Play to Help Your Child Through Difficult Times) describes how to help children heal from stress or trauma through play. As in Part 2, each chapter addresses a specific topic, so you can easily find useful tips for your personal family situation. You will learn which of the nine forms of play are particularly effective for each specific kind of stress or trauma.

In the first appendix, you will find summary charts describing each kind of play for easy reference. The second appendix provides a brief overview of the theoretical rationale for the various forms of attachment play. I have summarized some of the research findings showing their effectiveness in transforming children's challenging behaviors and emotions. A list of scientific references follows this appendix.

Part 1

Getting Started

"PLAY WITH ME, Mommy! Play with me, Daddy!" How often have you heard your children make this request? Children love to play, and they especially enjoy playing with their parents. When you play with your children, you meet their need for connection and help them feel loved. In fact play is one of the best ways to charge up your children's emotional batteries.

This section describes nine specific kinds of activities that are especially effective in strengthening the parent-child bond. I call these activities attachment play. Many of these forms of play also lie at the root of effective discipline as well as emotional healing. These are the forms of play that I recommend most frequently to parents who are struggling with their children's challenging behaviors or emotions.

Chapter 1

Introduction to Attachment Play

HEALTHY PARENT-CHILD ATTACHMENT is vital for children's emotional health, and parent-child social interaction plays a major role in promoting healthy attachment. When our children are babies, we connect with them through silly little activities such as peek-a-boo or pat-a-cake, and we playfully imitate their sounds, blow bubbles on their tummies, play with their toes, rock them to music, and bounce them on our knees. These daily mutual interactions help babies acquire a sense of confidence, trust, security, reciprocity, humor, and joy. When we engage babies in these playful activities while remaining sensitive and responsive to them, they learn to communicate and connect with us.

If you continue to interact playfully with your children as they grow older, you can maintain a healthy attachment with them. When they say "play with me," they will feel truly loved and valued if you sit on the floor to join them in their fantasy play with dolls, trains, or blocks. You will find endless opportunities for connecting playfully with your children by playing board games or just being silly together.

If your family is stressed by factors such as work, illness, divorce, financial difficulties, the birth of a baby, or a move to a new home, the connection between you and your children may suffer. The attachment may weaken during these difficult times because you might (understandably) run out of patience or lack sufficient time to spend with your children. When this disconnection occurs, your children may begin to feel insecure, anxious, lonely, and powerless, and their behavior may become more difficult. In fact, most discipline problems occur when children feel disconnected, powerless, insecure, or frightened.

Attachment play can be a powerful healing factor for these difficult times. Unfortunately, your children may need to play with you the most when you least feel like playing with them! However, if you can manage just 20 to 30 minutes of play per day, your children will benefit immensely. Remember, too, that it is never too late to engage your children in these forms of therapeutic play. You can play with your children at a later time to restore your connection and help them heal.

Laughter is an especially beneficial component of play. Research has shown that laughter can reduce tension, anxiety, and anger. By playing and laughing with your children, you can resolve many discipline problems and also help your children heal from stress or trauma. So laughing with your children or acting silly with them is never a waste of time!

Attachment play has a solid basis in scientific research. Findings from research studies support the effectiveness of these nine kinds of activities with children suffering from specific emotional and behavioral problems. (See Appendix B for a description of these studies.) However, attachment play can benefit *all* children, even those who are emotionally healthy and well behaved.

Attachment play has a unique set of characteristics, which differ from traditional games or sports. The following list describes these basic characteristics.

Characteristics of attachment play
What it is

- **Attachment play is interactive play that strengthens your connection to your children.**
  You will feel closer to your children after doing the activities in this book, and you will bring out the best in each other.

- **Attachment play often involves laughter.**
  You will laugh *with* your children, not *at* them. Laughter reduces tension, anxiety, and anger.

- **Attachment play can be either child initiated or adult initiated.**
  Your children may initiate attachment play themselves, and this book will help you recognize their invitations to play. You can also initiate these activities yourself to resolve specific discipline problems or help your children through difficult times.

- **Attachment play does not require any special equipment.**
  A major advantage of attachment play is that it's free! Many of the activities do not require any equipment at all, whereas others involve toys or objects that you probably already have in your home (such as dolls and pillows).

- **Attachment play can take place anywhere, at any time.**
  You can do these activities in the bathroom, in your car, on the playground, at the doctor's office, or at bedtime.

- **Attachment play includes many familiar activities.**
  If you play peek-a-boo with your baby, pretend to be frightened when your child growls like a lion, or find playful ways to deal with sibling rivalry, then you are already practicing attachment play.

What it isn't

- **Attachment play is not permissive discipline.**
  Attachment play can help you set limits and resolve common discipline problems. Your children will become more *willing* to cooperate, but they will not become "spoiled" or think that everything in life has to be fun.

- **Attachment play does not teach children to be aggressive.**
  Some of the forms of play described in this book encourage children to be physically active, but they will *not* cause your children to become more aggressive or hyperactive. On the contrary, they will make your children calmer, gentler, more compassionate, and more cooperative.

- **Attachment play is not a form of teasing.**
  These forms of play respect children and their feelings. They do not belittle children or make them feel incapable or inferior in any way. Instead, they will enhance your children's self-esteem and self-confidence.

- **Attachment play does not involve competition.**
  Contrary to most traditional games and sports, these activities have no winners or losers. The essential point is that everyone has a good time, and nobody feels like a loser. Everybody wins during attachment play.

- **Attachment play does not have any set rules.**
  These activities can change from one day to the next. You and your children may enjoy creating your own versions, which may differ from the descriptions in this book. Your invented games may even become your own unique family traditions.

Chapter 2

The Nine Forms of Attachment Play

THERE ARE NINE basic kinds of play that meet the characteristics described in Chapter 1. The following chart summarizes these activities, and the sections in this chapter describe each in more detail. You will find summary charts for each kind of play in Appendix A and research findings about these forms of play in Appendix B.

The nine forms of attachment play

- Nondirective child-centered play
- Symbolic play with specific props or themes
- Contingency play
- Nonsense play
- Separation games
- Power-reversal games
- Regression games
- Activities with body contact
- Cooperative games and activities

Nondirective child-centered play

I sat on the floor in the family's playroom and gave my full
attention to three-year-old Paul while his parents observed
us. He chose to play with blocks and soon built a small
house, announcing that the house had no toilet. He then
introduced a figure of a man who entered the house, and
said, "The man has to pee, but there's no toilet, so he wet his
pants!" He found this very funny and laughed while talking
about it.

Sometimes parents want me to play with their child before they
meet privately with me for a consulting session. During this play
time, I always use nondirective child-centered play because it's the
best way to become acquainted with a child. Within the first ten
minutes of play, children often bring up issues that are bothering
them. In the example above, I suspected that Paul and his parents
had some conflicts with toilet training. When I later met alone with
the parents, I asked them about this, and they told me that they had
indeed been having a struggle with toilet training.

To implement nondirective child-centered play, begin by providing materials that inspire your children to imagine, create, and
build, such as blocks, dolls, a doll house, puppets, clay (or play
dough), dress-up clothes, art supplies, small figures, animals, and
vehicles. Then let your child take the lead.

I recommend dedicating at least half an hour, once a week, to
engage each of your children in individual child-centered play sessions. This means that you will need to make caretaking arrangements for your other children if you have more than one. Daily play
sessions would be even better, if you have the time. To help your
child feel especially loved and valued, I recommend not answering
the telephone or otherwise distracting yourself during these special
play sessions. Your child may benefit even more from your attention
if you set a timer and tell your child that you will play with him until
it rings. Using a timer may also make it easier for you. Many parents
find that they are better able to pay attention to their child when
they know that it will end after a set amount of time.

When you begin to engage your child in nondirective play sessions, don't be surprised if he incorporates family conflicts, discipline issues, or past traumatic events into his play. This behavior is normal and healthy, and it indicates that he feels safe with you to share his conflicts and challenges.

Nondirective child-centered play helps children feel acknowledged, safe, and loved. It is especially useful for reconnecting after stress or separations, helping children heal from trauma, or simply strengthening your connection. If you have used harsh discipline in the past, or if there has been domestic violence in your home, the use of child-centered play sessions can help your child regain a sense of trust and safety.

Symbolic play with specific props or themes

At 18 months of age, my son developed a fear of dogs after a friendly puppy had jumped on him. One day, just for fun, I crawled on all fours and barked like a dog. He laughed hilariously and wanted me to do it again. We played this dog game for several days until his fear of dogs subsided.

Symbolic play with specific props or themes is especially effective for helping children heal from trauma. During this kind of play, you take a more directive role by offering specific toys or suggesting a play theme relating to the child's traumatic experience. For example, if a dog has bitten your child, you might offer your child a stuffed toy dog or pretend to be a dog, as in the preceding example. If there has been a fire in your neighborhood, and your child continues to act terrified, you can invite her to play with a toy fire engine, a play house, and small human figures. Part 3 of this book contains many examples of this kind of therapeutic play with children.

You can also use symbolic play to cope with behavior problems such as toilet training, sibling rivalry, lying, and lack of cooperation. By role playing specific conflicts with stuffed animals and other props, you can change your child's behavior. Part 2 explains how to use symbolic play for these specific discipline issues.

Contingency play

> I visited my granddaughter when she was two years old.
> She acted shy with me at first because we had not seen each
> other for several months. I sat on the floor and watched her
> while she played with some toys at a short distance from me.
> When she accidentally dropped a doll on the floor, I pre-
> tended to be the doll and said, "Ouch!" She giggled, picked
> up the doll, and purposely dropped it on the floor. Again,
> I said, "Ouch!" much to her delight. She threw the doll on
> the floor at least twenty more times, and I said, "Ouch!"
> each time while she laughed heartily. After this game, she
> no longer acted shy with me and willingly sat on my lap.

Contingency play is any activity in which the adult's behavior is
predictably repeated and contingent on the child's behavior. As the
example above illustrates, contingency games are a great way to
establish a warm connection with a child.

A favorite kind of contingency play with young children is a
piggy-back ride in which you follow your child's non-verbal instructions to turn right or left, or to stop. For example, you turn to the
right when your child taps your right shoulder and to the left when
he taps your left shoulder. Another favorite contingency activity
is the poking game. When your child pokes your right cheek, you
make a happy face, and when he pokes your left cheek, you make
a sad or angry face. If he pokes your hand, you start flapping it up
and down but stop as soon as he pokes it again. You can invent
additional movements involving other parts of your body.

Most children enjoy contingency play, which has an infinite
number of variations. The key element is that the adult's behavior
is contingent on the child's behavior. These games can promote
connection, enhance trust, convey acceptance, create a sense of
empowerment, and establish a reassuring feeling of predictability.
The laughter that occurs during these games helps children release
tensions resulting from anxiety, powerlessness, and loss of control
during previous traumatic experiences.

These activities counteract the chronic feeling of powerlessness that all children feel at times because they are smaller and less capable than adults. Children usually do not make the major decisions about where they live, where they attend school, or who takes care of them. Parents must control much of children's lives. When these adults use power-based methods of discipline (which I do *not* recommend), children feel even more powerless, manipulated, and controlled. During contingency play, children can feel for a moment that they are in control. After this kind of play, parents often notice that their children more willingly accept necessary limits and cooperate with parental requests.

Imitation games are a form a contingency play. You can begin to play imitation games when your infant first starts to verbalize sounds (other than crying). He will probably be delighted if you mimic his squealing or cooing. Imitation games can help children develop a sense of empathy. When your children see their own sounds and movements mirrored by you, they will learn to associate these cues with the specific emotional states that they themselves are feeling. This, in turn, will help them understand that other people have the same mental experiences that they have.

> When my daughter was seven months old, she loved it when I imitated her sounds. If she said "ga," I replied "ga." She would then repeat the sound while looking at me expectantly and smiling. We had delightful "conversations" of this nature.

A mother reported the following imitation game with her infant.

> Whenever my baby had the hiccups, I would attend closely and try to hiccup at the same time as he did, usually managing just after him, like an echo. Starting as early as five months of age, he found this hilarious, and it created a warm, bonded feeling between us every time.

Older children enjoy imitation games such as follow the leader or
Simon says, in which one child is the leader and the others must
follow and imitate.

Nonsense play

When my son was 20 months old, we were playing together,
and he suddenly pretended to blow his nose in his shirt
while looking at me and laughing heartily.

At eleven years of age, my son and his friends participated
in a school play, for which they had to memorize many lines
of spoken text as well as songs and dances. A few days after
the last performance, I drove my son and three other boys
from his class to a party. They spent the entire 15-minute car
ride reciting their memorized lines *incorrectly* while laughing hilariously. When I later commented on this to my son,
he informed me that he and his friends had been doing this
ever since the final performance.

Nonsense play is any play in which you or your child acts silly by
making obvious mistakes or by playfully exaggerating emotions or
conflicts. This kind of play qualifies as attachment play when it involves parent-child interaction. Either you or your child can initiate
this kind of play.

Children often initiate nonsense play that involves making
mistakes. Your child may put her pants on her head instead of on
her legs, purposely recite nursery rhymes incorrectly, or put puzzle
pieces in the wrong places. The laughter that occurs when children
spontaneously engage in these silly activities indicates a release of
tension.

When my son pretended to blow his nose in his shirt (in the
first example above), the source of his tension may have been an
accumulation of frustration resulting from all the times when I had
interrupted his play by holding a tissue to his nose and asking him
to blow into it. Perhaps he also felt some anxiety about meeting my
expectations for blowing his nose the correct way. He sensed that

this issue seemed important to me and was beginning to internalize that particular rule for behavior. Thus, doing the activity incorrectly (while I was watching) felt a little rebellious to him and seemed funny.

The second example above shows that older children also use nonsense play spontaneously. Reciting their memorized lines incorrectly helped the children release the stress resulting from stage fright, as well as their teacher's expectations to perform correctly. This kind of nonsense play is especially useful for children who are afraid of making mistakes. Perhaps they have been teased or punished for making mistakes in the past, have teachers with overly high expectations, or are perfectionists themselves.

Exaggeration is another form of nonsense play. You can use this approach to resolve discipline issues by playfully exaggerating conflicts to the point of becoming ridiculous or by inventing a silly game. Through the use of exaggeration and silliness, children can release pent-up anger or frustration through laughter. For example, if your eight-year-old daughter refuses to take a bath after playing at the beach, you could tell her playfully that you might have to use a bulldozer to remove all the sand from the floor (after it falls off her body) and then pretend to chase her with an imaginary bulldozer. Following this kind of play, children often cooperate much more willingly. In Part 2, you will find several examples of this version of nonsense play (exaggeration) to change your children's behavior.

You can also use exaggeration to help children work through fears. This approach is useful when the child is too overwhelmed by the real source of fear. In this case, you can encourage a display of exaggerated fear for some small aspect of the thing that frightens her. For example, if your child is terrified of snakes, you can both pretend to be terrified of the sound "S".

Separation games

At ten months of age, my son initiated a game of peek-a-boo by repeatedly putting a blanket over his head and then removing the blanket. Each time he removed it, I said "peek-a-boo" and he laughed heartily.

Separation games are activities in which you create a short visual or spatial separation between you and your child. These activities include the well-known games of peek-a-boo and hide-and-seek.

In the game of peek-a-boo, you briefly hide your own face or your baby's face and then suddenly reappear. Babies between six and eighteen months of age usually enjoy this game and laugh. As the example above illustrates, babies sometimes initiate the game. The tensions released through laughter are those resulting from separation anxiety, which peaks during that age range. This anxiety represents a normal, developmental fear present in securely-attached infants. When you play peek-a-boo with your baby, avoid staying hidden too long. Otherwise, your baby might fear that you have really disappeared.

Toddlers and older children enjoy the game of hide-and-seek and often laugh when you find them (or when they find you). As children grow older, the separations can last longer, and the hiding places can become gradually more challenging. Hide-and-seek has many variations. The important element in these games is the moment of visual and physical reconnection.

Chasing games are another kind of separation game. You can let your child run away from you and then try to catch him, or you can incorporate a chase into the game of hide-and-seek to prolong the separation and create more of a challenge. For example, when you discover your child's hiding place, let him escape and try to reach a (pre-designated) safe base before you catch him.

Separation games can help children deal playfully with daily separations such as going to daycare or school. They can also allow children to overcome frightening emotions resulting from past traumatic separations or loss, so they represent a form of symbolic play with a theme relating to the trauma. These games are also useful for children who have never suffered from traumatic separation or loss but who have an *imagined* fear of abandonment or separation. For example, some children develop a fear of abandonment after their parents get divorced, or after the children learn about kidnapping. In both cases, laughter during separation games can help the children release anxiety.

Power-reversal games

Five-year-old Eva noticed the plastic snakes and spiders among the toys in my office and started playing with them. I suggested that she could frighten her parents with them if she wished. She immediately pretended to have the animals bite her parents while they pretended to be frightened. Eva giggled and gleefully repeated the activity several more times. After she tired of this game, I gave her a small pillow and told her it was a magic pillow that would make her very strong if she held it. I said that it might even make her strong enough to knock her parents down. She immediately hit her parents with the pillow, and they toppled over onto the floor, pretending to be overpowered by the pillow. Eva laughed heartily and hit her parents several more times with the pillow. Then she picked up some large cloth scarves, laid them on top of her parents, and told them that they were frozen. Her parents obediently remained motionless until she removed the cloths. Finally, she discovered the doctor kit and proceeded to give "shots" to her parents while they pretended to be frightened. Eva loved the games and didn't want to leave when the session was over.

The above example is a description of a play session that I coached with a child and her parents. It illustrates several power-reversal games, including some that the child invented herself.

Power-reversal games are activities in which the adult pretends to be weak, frightened, clumsy, stupid, or angry. They are similar to contingency games, but they go beyond simply imitating the child or obeying the child's commands. The adult play acting is an essential component of power-reversal games.

Power-reversal games are often active. A typical example is a pillow fight in which you let your child knock you down with a pillow, as illustrated above. Your child doesn't really knock you down, of course. She simply hits (or touches) you with a pillow, and you play your part by faking weakness and falling down dramatically on the floor. Other kinds of power-reversal games involve burying the parent with pillows or blankets, pretending to lock up the parent in a cage, or using a magic wand to transform the parent into an animal or object.

The laughter during this kind of play is therapeutic because it helps the child release anxiety resulting from feelings of powerlessness. As mentioned in the section on contingency play, most children feel powerless at times simply because they are smaller and weaker than adults. This play can also help children heal from adult-inflicted trauma such as authoritarian discipline or abuse.

When I lead parent-child play days, we always begin with a 20-minute pillow fight between parents and their children. I instruct the parents to fake weakness and let their children knock them down. After one of these pillow fights during a workshop in Los Angeles, an eight-year-old girl announced enthusiastically, "This was better than Disneyland!"

Some parents fear that these games will increase their children's aggressive tendencies. However, the parents are amazed and delighted to discover that their children usually become much *less* aggressive and more cooperative after these activities. That's because the children have opportunities to release painful emotions of frustration, anger, anxiety, and powerlessness.

Mock terror is another effective response. My props for parent-child play coaching sessions include a collection of realistic-looking plastic spiders, snakes, and dinosaurs, as well as puppets representing a crocodile, wolf, and monster. The children love to frighten their parents with these toys.

In addition to faking weakness or fright, you can pretend to be clumsy or stupid. For example, you can play a chasing game in which you start to run away and invite your child to chase you. Then you pretend to stumble and then let your child catch you. If your child is swinging on a swing, you can stand in front of her and make clumsy attempts to catch her each time the swing approaches you. If you pretend that you cannot catch her before the swing takes her away, she will probably laugh.

You can also fake anger, as the following example illustrates.

At three years of age, my granddaughter enjoyed having me push her on a swing. While pushing her, I would stand in front of her and command her, with mock seriousness, *not* to kick me. Then I stood at the exact spot where her feet would touch me when the swing reached me. When her feet came close to me with each upward movement of the swing, I always jumped away just in time to avoid being kicked. Each time this occurred, I pretended to be angry and asked her to stop kicking me. She always laughed heartily. The fun part was that she knew that she was not really trying to kick me, and she understood that *I* knew this as well. This understanding between us created the necessary emotional safety for the game to be fun and therapeutic. The laughter may have helped her release feelings of powerlessness and frustration resulting from the fact that she is the youngest person in her extended family.

Children often initiate power-reversal games. If we can recognize these behaviors as invitations for play, we will help the children much more than if we dismiss or ignore the behaviors. A mother reported the following example to me of child-initiated power-reversal play with her three-year-old daughter.

I told my daughter that she could play with me after I had finished my e-mail. When I finally had some time to play with her, she pretended to type on an imaginary keyboard and replied, "I just have to write one more e-mail."

In this example, it's as if the child had said "let's pretend I'm the mother and you're the child, and I don't have time to play with you." It's possible that the girl simply wanted to feel momentarily powerful by making her mother wait a little. The mother could reply that she would be happy to wait until the e-mail has been sent. She could also enter into the play more actively by pretending to be upset and begging her daughter to play with her. This role-reversal would probably make her daughter laugh, thereby releasing some pent-up anger and frustration.

Regression games

Four-year-old Joanna began showing signs of stress when the parents went through financial difficulties and stress at work. The mother reported that Joanna acted sad and disconnected yet was quick to lash out in anger at her parents and also toward her friends. Her mother confessed to me that she herself had spoken harshly to Joanna and had not been emotionally available for her daughter. I suggested a game in which the parents could both pretend that Joanna was a baby while lovingly cuddling and rocking her, feeding her, and playing baby games with her. I also suggested that they should "fight" over whose turn it was to take care of her, ending up both holding and rocking her together. Later, the mother reported to me, "The consultation was very helpful. We have particularly enjoyed your suggestion to 'fight over the baby.' Joanna *beams* when we play this game. She is now requesting it and sets up little scenarios for us to enact. It is a wonderful contradiction for her, especially because my husband and I often hand her back and forth during the week. How wonderful to fight over her!"

Regression games include any play in which you engage your child in the kinds of activities that you would normally do with a younger child. Regression games are important for both connection and healing. Often, the children giggle during these regression games, but the games can be therapeutic even when the child does not laugh.

Children between the ages of three and six years of age often initiate regression play, and this behavior can be baffling and irritating for parents. Even an older child may sometimes pretend to be a younger child and use baby talk. In the following example, a mother describes her frustration and concern about her daughter's regression play:

> My daughter (age four) has started using baby talk. Normally, she talks very well and uses long sentences. But sometimes she says "I yike it" and "me want it." She will look at me with big eyes and say "up." And then the pout! She looks in the mirror to see how she appears with her mouth going down. And then she'll roll her eyes and pretend to cry like a baby. She has cultivated this incredible new image. I was so proud of her when she learned to talk earlier than other children, and now it upsets me when she acts like a baby!

There is no need to feel concerned if your child starts acting like a baby. I advised the mother in the example above to cradle her daughter in her arms, wrap her in a blanket, offer to feed her with a bottle, put imaginary diapers on her, sing lullabies, play with her toes, and so on.

An obvious time for regression play is after the birth of a sibling, when older children often feel displaced by the new baby. I have also recommended parent-initiated regression play for adoptive parents, as well as for mothers who suffered from illness or post-partum depression during their child's first year. It can also be useful during times of family stress when the adults have very little time or attention for the children, as in the first example above. By providing children with an experience of being lovingly nurtured like a baby, perhaps in ways that they never experienced before, this kind of play can help resolve trauma from early abuse, neglect, or separation. It gives them the kind of attention they needed when they were younger, and it strengthens them to grow and develop further.

Regression play can also be helpful after children take steps toward independence. In fact, children often start acting like a baby after accomplishing developmental milestones. By returning symbolically to babyhood, they can feel secure and loved while gaining confidence to continue moving toward independence. It's almost as if they need to recharge their batteries. Even older children sometimes use regression play, as the following example of my daughter illustrates.

At ten years of age, my daughter took a major step toward independence. She attended her first big slumber party with eight other girls. After returning home the following day, she pretended to be a baby and wanted to cuddle with me like a little baby.

Activities with body contact

I have a nephew who lives in another country, and whom I don't see very often. When he was three years old, I visited him and his family, and I naturally wanted to connect with him. However, he seemed reluctant to play with me because he didn't remember me. We went out to the family's large back yard, which was sloped, and he started running up and down the hill while totally ignoring me. After watching him do this a few times, I thought of a way to connect with him. I stood at the bottom of the slope and opened my arms wide, offering to catch him. He gleefully ran into my arms for a quick hug before returning to the top for another downhill run. He repeated this activity several times, and each time he arrived at the bottom, he chose to run into my waiting arms. After that activity, he treated me like an old friend.

An important function of play is its role in helping children connect physically with other people. If you encourage physical contact while respecting your child's boundaries, you will strengthen your connection. The shared enjoyment of playing and touching each other is a powerful factor that strengthens attachment and bonding. That's why play has the power to repair damaged parent-child relationships or those that have suffered from traumatic separations. When your children connect physically with you through play, they feel a sense of inherent worth, safety, and belonging. Being touched allows your children to become aware of their own bodies and feel good about their bodies. The child's reasoning is: "If mommy likes to cuddle with me, my body must be good." On the other hand, a child who is not touched or cuddled sufficiently might come to believe that his body is bad. This direct connection with you will also prevent feelings of isolation and alienation. Just as babies need to be held and touched by their parents, children continue to need physical contact as they grow older. In fact, touch remains a vital need throughout life.

The young of most land mammals have considerable contact with their mothers through suckling and snuggling close to the mother during sleep. This physical contact meets their needs for thermal regulation, protection, and nourishment. Many species of young mammals also engage in playful activities that involve physical contact with their mothers and siblings, such as playful wrestling or mutual grooming.

Human children seem to know intuitively that touch is important for optimal physical and emotional development. They enjoy being cuddled and held, and they will seek physical contact when frightened, tired, frustrated, hurt, or ill. Children also enjoy forms of play that incorporate body contact, such as playful wrestling or circle games in which they hold hands. They especially enjoy playful activities that involve physical contact with their parents.

Many of the games listed in this chapter involve body contact. You can look for additional ways to incorporate touch into playful activities with your children. When your children are little, you can bounce them on your knees, dance to music while holding them in your arms, play pat-a-cake, or give them piggy-back rides. When they are older, you can create an imaginary wheelbarrow by holding their ankles while they walk on their hands, or you can create a human sandwich by letting them lie on top of you. There are endless possibilities for playful body contact.

Cooperative games and activities

When my daughter was between the ages of eight and twelve years, we sometimes created a cooperative story while cuddling together at bedtime. To provide ideas, we had prepared cards with words in the following five categories: animals, people, places, magical beings, and magical objects. Before creating a story together, she would select, without looking, one card from each of these categories (for example, a crow, a queen, a tunnel, a dragon, and a magic golden arrow). Then we created a story together using those five elements, each person adding one sentence at a time. These cooperative stories helped us connect with each other and also allowed my daughter to relax before falling asleep.

Cooperative activities can strengthen your connection with your child. Children with vivid imaginations enjoy telling cooperative stories. Another enjoyable cooperative activity is to build a block tower as high as you can while taking turns placing one block on top of the other.

Playing games competitively can be fun, at times, and these activities can motivate children to do their very best, compare their skills to others, and measure their improvement. Cooperative games, however, offer opportunities for meaningful connection unhampered by the threat of losing. In cooperative games (also called noncompetitive games), everybody works toward a common goal, and nobody loses. It's therefore important to strike a balance between cooperative and competitive games.

Many cooperative board games exist, and you can also modify the rules of competitive board games so that nobody wins or loses. It's fun to play active cooperative group games at birthday parties. For example, you can modify the traditional party game, musical chairs, to make it non-competitive. In this variation, all the children sit on the chairs when the music stops, but nobody is excluded. As you gradually remove the chairs, the children must share them. When there is only one chair left, the children must cooperate to *all* sit on (or at least touch) the single chair. (Hopefully it's a big one!). Another cooperative party game is to keep several balloons in the air as long as possible.

Outdoor sports don't have to be competitive. You can modify the rules to create cooperative games in which everybody wins. For example, you can turn the games of ping pong or tennis into cooperative games by striving to hit the ball back and forth as many times as possible without missing.

When you cooperate toward a common goal with your child, whether it's a game or a real-life activity (such as a cooking project), you create a meaningful connection based on your child's natural desire to contribute, and you learn to recognize each other's strengths while bringing out the best in each other. These activities can help your child feel connected and valued. They are especially useful for eliciting cooperation, for dealing with children who cheat, and for behavior problems resulting from sibling rivalry or parental divorce.

Chapter 3

General Guidelines

THERE ARE SEVERAL important guidelines to keep in mind while using attachment play. These will enhance your effectiveness when you implement these activities with your children.

Follow your child's lead and remain flexible

The basic guideline for attachment play is to follow your child's lead. Children know what they need and usually ask for it, either directly or indirectly. When your children verbally beg you to play with them, you will know exactly what they want. But children sometimes use more subtle or indirect (and sometimes exasperating) behaviors to invite you to play with them. At those times, you may need to look beneath the surface to decipher the underlying message.

If your two-year-old daughter puts her socks on her hands instead of her feet, she may enjoy some nonsense play. When your four-year-old child pretends to be a baby, this may be a cue for you to engage him in regression play. If your six-year-old son shoots an imaginary gun at you, he is probably ready for a power-reversal game. If your twelve-year-old criticizes you when you try to keep score during a game of ping-pong, she may welcome a cooperative version of the game or even a silly, power-reversal version in which you fake incompetence. In all of these situations, your children are inviting you to play with them in specific ways so they can resolve difficult emotions. This book will help you learn to recognize your children's indirect invitations to play with you in these ways and teach you how best to respond.

There will be times when you will want to initiate some of these activities, especially for resolving discipline issues or helping children heal from a traumatic experience. When you initiate the play, observe your child carefully to see whether he engages in the play or withdraws. If he doesn't want to play, you can try to modify the activity. However, be aware of the possibility that your approach may be too direct, or your child may resist because he senses your hidden agenda. You can always return to more nondirective child-centered play sessions to restore a feeling of safety and trust.

If, on the other hand, your child is fully engaged in an activity and enjoying it, then it will probably be beneficial even if it's different from your original plan or the description in this book. I urge you to remain flexible because there is no single, correct way to do these activities. So be sure to follow your child's lead. What begins as symbolic play may turn into an active power-reversal game. When your child wants to stop playing, there is no point in prolonging the activity. Most of the time, however, you will probably discover that you become bored with these games much sooner than your children!

Avoid teaching or correcting your child

Unless you are using play to help your child with a homework assignment, it's important to avoid direct instruction during these activities. You will have plenty of other opportunities to teach your child. The goal of attachment play is to help your child express what she is feeling and to strengthen your connection with her. Teaching and correcting her will not contribute toward these goals. Try to accept everything your child does during attachment play, unless she is being hurtful toward another person, an animal, or the environment.

For example, if your child spontaneously sorts blocks by color, you can casually mention: "I see that you've put the red blocks over here and the blue blocks over there." But avoid saying: "These are red. Can you say that? RED." If your child sorts them incorrectly, refrain from correcting her.

If your child re-enacts an emergency trip to the hospital during symbolic play, let her supply whatever details she wants even if they do not reflect the reality of what actually happened. If she acts out a scene in which a mommy figure accompanies a child figure in a toy ambulance, don't remind her that mommy did not ride in the ambulance. Perhaps she *wishes* her mommy had been there and is expressing this wish through play.

Avoid interpreting or analyzing your child's play

Your attention and participation in your child's play are sufficient. There is no need to verbally analyze the underlying meaning. Although you may want to make your own private interpretations, and perhaps even discuss them with your partner, your child will probably not benefit from hearing them.

For example, if your child wants to play hide-and-seek with you repeatedly after you were hospitalized for a week, you may suspect that he needs to play this separation game in order to overcome the traumatic impact on him of your hospitalization. However, he does not need to hear your interpretation. That's because language and emotions are processed in different parts of the brain, with few nerve connections between them, especially in young children. Your child's desire to play hide-and-seek is his way of telling you that he needs to "work on" that difficult time, and your participation in the play will allow him to feel acknowledged and understood. If you try to shift your child's focus away from play by encouraging him to talk or by verbally interpreting his behavior, you might inadvertently interrupt your child's healing process.

As children grow older, they acquire the ability to process emotions by talking. Symbolic play, in particular, will gradually give way to language, but it's best to let your child initiate the dialog. For example, a ten-year-old might verbally express a fear of separation instead of engaging you in a game of hide-and-seek. Even when your child talks, however, it's best to refrain from giving interpretations. If you can listen attentively without analyzing your children's emotions, they will feel understood and will work through their emotions.

Even though symbolic play eventually becomes replaced by language, older children (including teenagers!) can continue to benefit from many other forms of attachment play, such as a power-reversal arm wrestling game or playful exaggeration and silliness (nonsense play). Remember, too, that talking can never replace the need to laugh or cry.

If your child is laughing, you are probably on the right track

Encouraging laughter is another basic guideline. Laughter often occurs when there is an element of fear, embarrassment, frustration, or anger, but enough emotional safety so that the child does not feel threatened or frightened. When your child laughs during these various forms of play, it probably means that she is feeling safe enough to release tensions. A good balance between safety and tension is the key to successful play.

If you are using a crocodile puppet to help your four-year-old son overcome a fear of crocodiles (symbolic play), and if he appears to be afraid of the puppet and stops laughing, you will need to change the activity. You could pretend that the puppet is a baby crocodile who is frightened of *him* and who hides under the bed for protection. Likewise, if you are having a playful pillow fight with your daughter, and she stops laughing while beginning to fight "for real," it's time to switch your approach because the play has become too serious and no longer therapeutic. Her laughter may resume if you direct her aggression toward a doll and then provide dramatic sound effects of screeching agony each time she hits the doll.

Sometimes young children need reassurance about the symbolic nature of these activities. If your three-year-old daughter wears a lion mask and roars, she will probably giggle if you pretend to be frightened (a power-reversal game). However, if you are too dramatic in your play acting, she may stop laughing and feel the need to reassure you that she is not really a lion! This is a cue for you to act slightly less convincing in your role of the frightened parent.

Avoid teasing your child

During these activities, as in all forms of interaction with your children, it's important for your children to understand that you are not making fun of them or their emotions. Although laughter is generally therapeutic, some laughter-producing activities are not beneficial and can even be harmful. Teasing is one of these harmful activities. Sometimes children (and adults) laugh when they are teased because the situation creates *new* feelings of embarrassment, powerlessness, or oppression. This is *nervous* laughter, as opposed to *therapeutic* laughter.

It is disrespectful to make fun of children for their imperfections or emotions. Teasing can damage the bond you have with your children. When you make fun of your children, no matter how humorously you do it, their self-esteem will be diminished. If your son cries easily, don't call him the family's "water fountain." If you are disturbed or embarrassed by his tears, take the time to explore your emotions with another adult, away from your child. Perhaps you cried easily when you were a child and your own parents teased you, so you find yourself repeating the same words without thinking. Perhaps you worry that other people will not like your child or that he won't be able to cope with life's challenges. When you discover the underlying reasons for your urge to tease, you will find it easier to resist teasing or even commenting on your child's behavior.

Imitative contingency play can easily turn into a form of teasing. Your children may enjoy it when you copy their sounds or movements in certain situations, but there is a risk that they may feel mocked. So try to be sensitive to your child's feelings when you use playful imitation.

Children love humor that involves exaggerating and silly mistakes (nonsense play). The laughter in these situations is generally therapeutic because it reduces the tension children feel about failing to meet adult expectations or about having necessary restrictions placed on their behavior. Like imitation, however, this kind of play also runs the risk of causing harm if the child feels mocked.

A possible indication that your child feels mocked is if he no longer wants to play (even though he may have been laughing). You can also ask your child afterwards if he enjoyed the activity, or you can judge the effectiveness of the play by his behavior. If he seems more relaxed, self-confident, cooperative, and connected to you, then the play was probably beneficial. However, if he seems tense, withdrawn, angry, insecure, or uncooperative, then you may need to modify the way you play.

Avoid tickling your child

Tickling is another activity that brings laughter, but it can be harmful. That's because tickling, like teasing, is a form of attack, and it can create feelings of powerlessness. When you tickle a child, you are essentially dominating her. Although babies and children usually laugh when you tickle them, this laughter may be a release of the fear and powerlessness *caused* by the tickling.

Some parents feel confused when their children ask to be tickled. There are times when tickling may be harmless, especially when it's part of a song or nursery rhyme, and the child expects it. In these situations, your child may enjoy being tickled briefly because she has time to prepare herself for it and knows that you will not prolong it against her will. Expected tickling provides a much different experience from unexpected tickling.

When your child asks to be tickled, consider the possibility that this request may be the only way she knows to obtain physical connection with you. Perhaps she uses the word "tickle" to mean gentle stroking on her arms or legs. By providing her with this form of touch, you will meet her need. You could also suggest other ways to be close, perhaps by cuddling with her or giving her a back rub.

Another way to respond is to suggest a power-reversal game. For example, you can play the role of a clumsy tickling monster who never manages actually to catch and tickle the child. Or you could do the ticking motions without actually touching your child. Another possibility is to invite your child to be the tickling monster who chases *you*. Of course, you must play your part by letting your child catch and tickle you. Your children will probably enjoy these empowering games much more than an activity in which you actually tickle them.

Don't try these activities when your child is crying

Crying is an important stress-release mechanism, just like play and laughter. I recommend offering comfort and support to a crying child while letting the outburst run its course. This is not a good time to initiate a playful activity. In fact, it would be disrespectful to distract a crying child with a game. Your children need you to acknowledge and accept their emotions, even the most painful ones. It's not your job to decide what feelings your children should have, but it *is* your job to provide love and acceptance no matter what your children are feeling. If you try to shorten your child's crying with a playful activity, he may stop crying temporarily but will probably attempt to resume his crying at a later time.

Raging and tantrums are also important stress-release mechanisms. These meltdowns represent a healthy release of accumulated frustration or anger. After a good tantrum, children are usually calm, relaxed, and cooperative. When your child has a temper tantrum, try to stay close without distracting or scolding him, even when this requires an enormous amount of patience. Your child needs to know that the bond between you is stronger than his anger. Rest assured, your child is not trying to manipulate you, nor is he spoiled.

Sometimes setting a limit with children can precipitate a tantrum. If you have set a reasonable limit (such as telling your child that you will not buy a toy for him that day), and your child begins to scream and rage, there is no need to give in and change your mind. However, your child has the right to express his emotions, and he needs your support.

If your child cries during or after a parent-child playful activity, this does not necessarily imply that you have done something wrong. Sometimes a small pretext will unleash the tears. Perhaps he bumps his head during a playful pillow fight (power-reversal game). If you pay attention to him, he will seize the opportunity to unload not only the physical pain but also a burden of stress that has been accumulating. Or maybe you have just spent a half hour playfully interacting with your child during his evening bath. Later, when it's time to brush his teeth, he has a full-blown meltdown because you bought the wrong kind of tooth paste. This tantrum probably has nothing to do with the tooth paste, which is only a trigger for releasing deeper frustrations. I call this kind of tantrum the "broken-cookie phenomenon." Interestingly, children often cry *more* after they receive good quality attention. That's because they have soaked up so much love that they feel safe to release deeper, painful emotions. My book, *Tears and Tantrums*, has more information about crying.

Seek professional therapy for major traumas

I don't recommend play to help your child through major traumas such as sexual abuse or the death of a family member. Instead, I suggest that you seek professional therapy for your child (or your entire family) if your child has experienced such major traumas.

There are three reasons for this recommendation. First of all, play may not be the best way to help a child who is traumatized by sexual abuse or death. Your child may need to cry or express anger, and a supportive environment for these intense emotions may be more effective than a playful approach. Secondly, you will probably also be traumatized, and it would be difficult for you to feel objective enough to engage your child in therapeutic play. Thirdly, there is always a risk of re-traumatizing a child, especially with the use of symbolic play that triggers the trauma in a playful context. Professional therapists would know when and how to use play in these situations.

In addition to these two major traumas, there may be other events that lead to symptoms of post-traumatic stress in your children, and professional therapy may also be advisable in these situations. Don't hesitate to seek help whenever you feel concerned about your child's behavior. The advice in this book is not meant to replace professional advice or treatment.

It's okay to say that you don't want to play

There will be times when you won't have the desire, time, or energy to play with your children even though they are begging you to do so. It's okay to tell your children that you don't want to play or are unable to do so at those times. There is no harm in teaching your children that you are not always available. Try to find other interesting activities for them to do on their own, and then play with them later when you have more time or energy. But be sure to keep your promises. If you tell your daughter that you will play with her after dinner, don't change your mind.

Another way to meet both of your needs is to involve your children in your activities. This approach works especially well with chores around the home. If you need to cook dinner or sort the laundry, for example, invite your children to help if they are old enough. You can even try to make these activities fun and playful.

If you sacrifice your own needs and play with your children more than you really want to, they will probably enjoy all the attention you give them, but the risk of self-sacrifice is that you may begin to resent your children. Your resentment may then express itself through impatient or angry behavior toward them. This reaction of yours will cause your children to feel frightened and insecure, which will lead to even more clinging and demanding behavior. So ironically, the more you play with your children out of a sense of duty, the more demanding they may become! On the other hand, if you ignore your children and fail to meet their needs for quality interactive play, they may feel resentful, unloved, and insecure. Children have legitimate needs for attention and playful interactions, and they thrive when these needs are met. So try to meet everyone's needs by striking a balance between child-centered and adult-centered activities. The next chapter discusses various reasons why you may find it difficult to play with your children.

Chapter 4

When You Find It Hard to Play

A MOTHER I interviewed described how difficult it was for her to play with her daughter:

> I'm not real good at humor and laughter. It's my last thought. At the end of the day, I'll think: "Gosh, we could have laughed at that. We could have used humor." I have no idea how to do that. When Clara (age four) is humorous and laughing at home, I tend to interpret that behavior as out of control and a waste of time. It's usually around bedtime, and that's when I'm the least tolerant. And then my husband will come home, and he's been working all day at serious things, and he's wonderful and humorous and joyous. I kind of hate him for it. It makes me feel terrible when he can be so fun loving because it's hard for me to be that way. So I just leave the room and let him and Clara be humorous together. But he has his limits. Last Saturday, he and Clara played and did silly things to the point where he got fed up, and I could hear him getting tense. I realized that even the best people reach their limits!

Even the most patient parent sometimes lacks the motivation for play. A father said to me, "When it's 95 degrees, and I'm dripping with sweat, and my four-year-old is refusing to get in her car seat for the third time that day, I just don't feel like playing. I don't have the energy to think up some creative, playful way to get her to cooperate!" Don't be hard on yourself if you feel unable to play with your children during these difficult moments. This book will provide you with a wealth of play ideas, including techniques for eliciting cooperation in your children, but it cannot control the weather!

Sometimes deeper reasons can interfere with your good intentions to play. If you don't enjoy playing with your children, perhaps it's because your parents never played with you. Maybe you have unpleasant childhood memories associated with play. Or maybe you suffer from chronic depression or anxiety and simply cannot bring yourself to sit on the floor and do silly things with your children. Perhaps you feel bored while playing or resent the time and attention you give to your children because you don't have enough time for yourself or your other relationships. Maybe your work schedule leaves you exhausted, with little time for your children. Perhaps you simply don't know how to interact in fun ways with children. Whenever you or your family is going through difficult times, you will find it especially difficult to play with your children.

If you feel that some deeper, personal obstacles (such as the ones listed above) are getting in your way of playing with your children, the following exercises may make it easier for you to do so. These exercises will give you an opportunity to look for connections between your childhood experiences and your current feelings about your children and play. They will also encourage you to meet your own needs.

Remember that it's never too late to initiate attachment play even if you missed opportunities to play with your children in the past. Remember, too, that the more you play with your children, the more skilled you will become, and the more you will enjoy it. You and your children will begin to feel more connected, and your power struggles will decrease. When your children are grown, all of you will cherish pleasant memories of playing and laughing together.

Exercises

Explore your childhood

Take the time to talk with another adult (away from your children) about your childhood memories of playing. Writing in a journal can also be an effective way to explore your childhood. Here are some questions to get you started:

1. What was your favorite toy as a child? What did you enjoy doing with it? With whom?

2. Is there a specific toy that you wanted but never received? What was it? Where did you see it?

3. What was your favorite game as a child? Who did you play it with? How did it make you feel?

4. Recall a time when your mother or father played with you. What game? How did you feel about it? Was it pleasant or disagreeable? Do you wish that they had played more with you?

5. What memories do you have associated with competition? How did you feel when you won a game? When you lost a game?

6. Did anybody ever criticize you for the way you played or for the toys that you chose to play with?

Express your feelings about your children

1. Of the following statements, which ones reflect how you feel about your children? Take the time to express your emotions (with another adult or through writing) and to explore the origin of these feelings.

   - I enjoy playing with my child.
   - I feel irritated when my child asks me repeatedly to play with him.
   - I wish my child would play more alone.
   - I wish my child would let me play more with him.
   - I feel upset because my child always likes to win games.
   - I feel upset when my child makes up his own rules.
   - I feel irritated when my child cheats at a game.
   - I become impatient when my child acts silly.
   - I get bored playing the same games repeatedly.
   - I worry about my child's choice of toys.
   - I worry my child has too many (or not enough) toys.
   - Other feelings?

2. Give your child your complete, undivided attention for half an hour and let him decide what to do. Join in the play if he invites you, but avoid directing the play in any way. Try to be aware of your feelings during this time. Later, talk to someone about your feelings or write them down in a journal.

Nurture yourself

1. Are your basic needs being met? Look at the list below and mark the ones that are not getting met. Then try to think of concrete steps you can take to meet these legitimate needs.

   - Time alone
   - Time with your spouse or partner
   - Cuddling/touching/sex
   - Time for play/leisure activities
   - Rest/sleep
   - Nourishing food
   - Exercise
   - Meaningful work
   - Connection with a larger community (family or friends)
   - Being listened to
   - Opportunities to release emotions (talking, laughing, crying)
   - Support for your work of parenting
   - Other needs?

2. Join with other families to form playgroups or support groups. You don't have to raise your children in isolation.

3. What kind of play or leisure activity nurtures you as an adult? (ex: tennis, chess, card games, dancing, hiking, singing, films, etc.) Try to schedule some of those leisure activities into your life (with or without your children).

Part 2

Using Attachment Play to Solve Discipline Problems

PLAY AND LAUGHTER can be wonderful tools for resolving discipline problems. In this section, you will find a variety of playful techniques for dealing with typical conflicts. These activities will help you set limits and elicit cooperation in your children without the use of either punishments or rewards.

Children who are struggling with stress or unhealed trauma often act aggressively, resist bedtime, or refuse to cooperate. Helping children heal from stress is therefore an important part of nonpunitive discipline. Part 3 describes how to use attachment play to help children through difficult times and heal from trauma, so some of those chapters may also be relevant for the specific discipline issues that you are facing.

Chapter 1

Introduction to Non-Punitive Discipline

SOME PARENTS HESITATE to use play to resolve conflicts with their children, because they think of discipline as a serious topic, and they fear that a playful approach will only reinforce undesirable behavior. These parents think that their job is to set rules, enforce consequences, and teach their children to obey. However, obedience training requires the use of punishment and has numerous pitfalls.

Research has shown that physical punishment, such as spanking, harms children, increases aggressive behavior, and can lead to later anxiety or depression. But even nonviolent consequences, such as time-out or loss of privileges, have numerous pitfalls. For example, the use of time-out can cause children to feel abandoned at times when they most need to feel loved and connected. Furthermore, these consequences fail to address the underlying causes of children's behavior.

Although it is possible to turn children into obedient little people by threatening them with painful consequences, this kind of obedience is not the joyful, heart-felt cooperation that specific forms of play can elicit. Anyone with more power can force someone with less power to obey, and this certainly holds true for parents and children. But what is your real goal? And what kind of relationship do you want with your children?

A major problem with the use of punishment (both violent and nonviolent) is that it can damage your relationship with your children, and they may begin to resent you. Many children rebel during adolescence, but not all children do. Those who have been raised with a non-punitive approach to discipline are much less likely to rebel. Teenagers typically begin to question their parents' values and lifestyle in order to forge their own identity, but this individuation process can occur while maintaining a close, loving connection to the parents without any overt rebellion.

Some parents refrain from punitive discipline but try to motivate their children with hugs, gold stars, ice cream, special privileges, and other goodies. Although this approach is kinder than a punitive one, reward systems also have several pitfalls. One problem with rewards is that you will eventually run out of them as your children grow older and become less dependent on you. For example, the promise of a special treat loses its motivational power when your children can buy these treats for themselves.

Another problem is that the use of rewards can backfire because it can change your children's *reason* for complying. Your children may do what you want simply to obtain the promised reward rather than meet your needs or the needs of the family. External motivators can therefore undermine your children's developing sense of cooperation and altruism. Later, when you no longer offer rewards, your children may see no reason to comply, because they have become dependent on these external motivators. They may even have failed to acquire the values that you want them to have.

Numerous studies have demonstrated this disadvantage of reward systems, which tend to reduce what psychologists call *intrinsic motivation*. Children who learn to do things for external rewards become dependent on others to control their behavior and may even stop using good judgment. This can lead to unfortunate situations later on. As these children grow older, they may switch their allegiance to someone who offers more interesting rewards than your gold stars without bothering to question the honesty or integrity of such a person.

Before trying to change your child's behavior, ask yourself the following two questions: "How do I want my child to behave?" and

"What do I want my child's *motivation* to be for this behavior?" The following examples illustrate two different kinds of motivation.

- Do you want your four-year old daughter to refrain from pulling the cat's tail to avoid being put in time-out? Or because she respects animals?

- Do you want your six-year-old son to set the table in order to receive a gold star for the day and a prize at the end of the week? Or because he feels part of the family and wants to contribute?

- Do you want your eight-year-old daughter to read books to earn gold stars or good grades in school? Or because she enjoys reading?

- Do you want your ten-year-old son to clean up his room so you will allow him to watch TV? Or because he values beauty and order?

- Do you want your children to treat each other nicely because they are afraid of being sent to their rooms if they fight? Or because they truly love each other and don't want to hurt each other?

A playful approach to discipline is one of several components involved in a non-punitive, democratic approach. The suggestions in this section will help you avoid the use of punishments and rewards while maintaining a good relationship with your children and decreasing their need for rebellion later on. This is a child-centered approach, but it is not a permissive one. In fact, it will increase your ability to set necessary limits and win your children's cooperation. Furthermore, you will be able to accomplish these goals while transmitting the real values and good judgment that you want your children to have.

The goal of discipline is to keep your children safe, give them the information they need to make wise choices in life, and teach them to think about the long-term consequences of their behavior (not artificial consequences that you create, but *real-life* consequences). Effective discipline builds on a strong parent-child connection and on children's inherent desire to belong, contribute, and learn.

Non-punitive discipline does not involve quick fixes or ready-made solutions. Each conflict is unique, and each requires a creative solution that fits the situation. This approach requires more patience and effort than the use of punishments or rewards, but the results will be well worth your efforts. If you avoid power-based methods of control and treat your children with love and respect, they will willingly cooperate with you and show compassion to others.

Chapter 2

Eliciting Cooperation

PLAY CAN BE a useful technique for eliciting cooperation with young children. Starting around 15 months of age, children enter a stage of autonomy, which can last for several years. During this stage, their favorite word is "no." Your 18-month-old daughter might run in the opposite direction when you announce that it's time to change her diaper. Your three-year-old son may refuse to use the toilet before getting in the car even though you know he has to urinate. Even older children may resist parental commands. If you tell your eight-year-old to get dressed or your twelve-year-old to clean up the living room, they may act as if they didn't even hear you. Many parents feel frustrated and challenged by these stubborn behaviors.

You may feel tempted to use a punitive approach. However, if you threaten your children with time-out, loss of privileges, or any other kind of punishment, you may gain temporary compliance but at a cost to your relationship with your children. Furthermore, your children are likely to rebel against your authority just as soon as they can, probably around the age of 13 years if not sooner.

Some parents go to the other extreme. They try to elicit cooperation in young children by explaining their own needs and then politely requesting compliance. At a playground, for example, a mother might say to her two-year-old: "It's time to go home now because I need to make dinner. Would you be willing to climb into your stroller?" This polite approach may gain compliance from adults, but it usually doesn't work very well with young children. A child who does not want to stop playing will simply respond "no" and continue to play. This is an honest reply to the mother's request. You can prevent this problem if you refrain from giving your children a choice about the specific behavior that you want them to do. If something is not negotiable, there is no point in using language that gives children the illusion of choice and the freedom to refuse. However, you can use playful ways to elicit cooperation with your children.

When there is an immediate conflict

Children find many of the things that we want them to do either boring or disagreeable. They have no inherent need to brush their teeth, sit in a car seat, put toys away, or take a bath. With young children, there are three ways to encourage cooperation without the use of either punishments or rewards: give explanations, give choices, and make it fun.

First of all, it's important to give explanations and reasons. Tell your children *why* you want them to comply with your requests, for example: "It's much safer for you to be in your car seat. I worry that you might bump your head if I have to stop the car suddenly."

Secondly, it's always useful to offer choices because they allow children to feel less controlled and more autonomous. Here are some examples of choices: "Do you want to wear your red shirt or your blue shirt?" "Do you want Mommy or Daddy to brush your teeth tonight?" "What snack would you like to take with you in the car?" Note that these examples do *not* give children a choice about whether or not to get dressed, brush teeth, or climb into the car, because those behaviors are not negotiable. The choices are for *other* things. This approach can increase children's willingness to comply.

Finally, you can make the activity fun, and this is where the play comes in. The basic idea is to "win" your child over to your side. If you can turn the activity into a game, your children will be more willing to cooperate with you. The following two examples from my own children illustrate playful ways to elicit cooperation.

> When Nicky was two years old, he enjoyed pretending that a mouse puppet had feelings and needs. When Nicky was hungry, Mousie wanted to eat too. When I read a book to

Nicky, I had to read to Mousie as well. This gave me the idea of using the mouse puppet to ask Nicky to do things. When I held the puppet on my hand and used a squeaky voice to ask him to do something (like brush teeth), he usually complied willingly.

At the age of four, Sarah often refused to use the toilet before we left home to go somewhere. When I asked her to use the toilet, she stubbornly refused my request while claiming that she didn't have to pee. I invented a game in which the goal was for her to finish urinating before I reached the end of the alphabet. I would begin reciting the alphabet, and when I reached the letter P, I would emphasize it, saying "peeeeeee…" loudly, much to her delight. After I had played this game a few times with her, she always ran to the toilet when I said "let's play alphabet pee pee." While reciting the alphabet, I always slowed down if necessary, so she could finish urinating before I reached the letter Z.

A mother shared the following example to illustrate how she uses a playful approach to encourage her son to help put toys away.

My son (age five) does not enjoy putting his toys away. I often create a game by announcing loudly, in a playful voice, that I will get the most blocks into the box. Then I start quickly putting them in the box with a gleeful look on my face. He always scrambles madly to beat me at it, and I lament loudly about how unfair it is that he is so fast. I complain that I hardly *ever* get to put away any blocks.

The following example illustrates my use of all three approaches for eliciting cooperation (giving explanations, giving choices, and being playful).

I was leading a playgroup for parents with their two-year-old children, and I had given the parents a hand-out that summarized ways to elicit cooperation in toddlers. Later, a little girl called Susie was playing in the outside sand area with a plastic doll house, and she refused to bring it inside at clean-up time when her mother asked her to do so. The mother asked me for help, so I went over to Susie, squatted down to her level, and said, "It looks like you are having fun with the doll house, but it's clean-up time and we need to put the doll house inside the room. I'm hungry and I want to go home to have lunch, but I can't leave until all the toys are inside" (explanations and reasons). Then I said, "Shall we sing a song while we put it away?" (playful activity). "Okay," she replied. Then I asked, "What song would you like to sing?" (choice). "Twinkle, Twinkle, Little Star," she replied. I continued, "Okay, we'll sing that song. Do you want to carry it by yourself, or do you want me to carry it?" (another choice). "I'll carry it," she replied. Susie then cheerfully carried the doll house inside the room and put it away while we sang the song together. Watching us, Susie's mother said to me, "That was amazing!" She had rarely seen her daughter cooperate so willingly.

Playful ways to elicit cooperation in young children (when there is an immediate conflict)

- Play a game: "Let's pretend we're horses galloping to the car."

- Use music: "It's time to sing our clean-up song."

- Tell a story: "I'll tell you a story while you take a bath."

- Provide a cooperative speed challenge or goal: "Let's surprise Daddy by straightening up the living room before he comes home."

- Suggest a competition, but use power-reversal and let the child win: "I bet I can put more blocks away than you!"

- Suggest a creative activity: "Let's make up a story while you put your pajamas on."

- Use a puppet: "Mousie says it's time to get dressed."

- Allow time for nonsense and silliness: "It's time to get dressed. Shall we put your socks on your hands?"

- Do it together by taking turns: "It's time to clear the table. Let's take turns removing one thing at a time. Do you want to start?"

- Do it together, simultaneously: "I'll sweep this half of the floor while you sweep the other half. We'll make a pile of dirt in the middle, and our brooms can say hello to each other."

You can modify these suggestions for older children to make them age appropriate. Don't assume that your children are too old to respond to playful suggestions. Instead, look for opportunities to engage them in play. Here's an example of the use of play with older children.

At ten years of age, my daughter participated in a Girl Scout weekend camp, which I attended as a helper. The scout group contained twenty girls between the ages of ten and twelve years. When we arrived at the camp lodge, we joined other groups in a large room. While waiting for the announcements to begin, the hundred girls in the room ran around, laughing and screaming. Amidst this chaos, I began to wonder why I had agreed to come! The adult leader of our group asked the girls to sit down and be quiet, but only a few of them obeyed her. As I watched the leaders become increasingly impatient and frustrated, I sat on the floor cross-legged and began clapping my hands in a regular rhythm, alternately clapping them together and on my thighs. I didn't say a word, but soon a few girls sat down near me and joined in the rhythmic clapping. As more girls spontaneously sat down and joined in, I invited them to form a circle. When all twenty girls were sitting in the circle, clapping in rhythm with me, I taught them to play a cooperative rhythm game. Soon all the girls in our group were enjoying the game. As the other groups watched ours, they began to calm down as well. We continued playing the game until the announcements began.

When there is no immediate conflict

The previous suggestions describe ways to elicit cooperation at the moment you are experiencing a conflict with your child. Another approach is to playfully bring up the conflict when it is *not* happening. Many conflicts with children occur repeatedly, and it can be useful to incorporate these themes into playful activities. When you are not caught up in the immediate need for your child to cooperate, both you and your child will feel more relaxed, objective, and free to think of creative solutions. The techniques for bringing up a conflict when it is not happening vary according to the child's age.

Birth to two years. With very young children, you can find ways to bring up a conflict when it is not happening by setting up a playful situation with the actual objects involved in the conflict. Here's an example.

At ten months of age, Marco did not like to sit in his car seat, and his father struggled with him each time he had to put him in it. The father had tried several playful approaches, but they worked only temporarily. I told the father to bring the car seat inside their home and place it on the living room floor. I advised him to let Marco crawl around it, explore it, and climb into it by himself. I also suggested playing peek-a-boo behind the car seat or crawling around it with his son in a mock chasing game. After a few days of these playful activities, Marco was much more willing to sit in his car seat when it was time to get in the car. The free play had empowered him and allowed him to release his feelings of frustration and anger through laughter while creating pleasant associations with the car seat.

Likewise, if your baby refuses to let you brush her teeth, you can let her play freely with her tooth brush at a time when you are *not* trying to brush her teeth. For example, you can hand it to her while she is sitting in a high chair. If she loses interest in it, you can invent silly little activities to play with it. For example, make a squeaky sound whenever she touches your nose with it (contingency play).

Uncooperative behavior can have its roots in unhealed trauma. One of my clients had an 18-month-old boy who refused to be strapped into his car seat and repeatedly resisted the physical confinement more than most children his age. Before birth, the umbilical cord had been wrapped around his head and one arm, preventing freedom of movement in utero and leading to the need for an emergency Cesarean. His parents were convinced that the car seat triggered a body memory of this early trauma. In such cases, the laughter play described above can be especially effective. (See Part 3 for more information about helping children heal from birth trauma.)

Uncooperative behavior can also simply be a need for a toddler to assert herself. This need first arises around 15 months of age when children's favorite word is "no." This is a good age to begin playing power-reversal games, which will help your toddler release emotions about feeling powerless in a world that is so often controlled by adults. Playing these games will make your toddler more willing to comply with your wishes. Although you are not bringing up any specific conflict, you are addressing the deeper issue of cooperation itself.

I began to play simple power-reversal games when my son was a toddler. Here's an example.

When my son reached 15 months of age, he began to run in the opposite direction whenever I told him that it was time to change his diaper. He also refused to let me dress him, although he was not yet able to do it himself. I decided that it was time to begin playing power-reversal games with him. While sitting next to him on a bed one day, I playfully and gently pushed him over to demonstrate what to do, and then I invited him to push *me* over. When he gave me a little push, I faked weakness and immediately fell over onto the bed. This caused him to laugh and eagerly repeat the action several times. We played this game often, and I noticed that he was usually more cooperative after these play sessions.

Two to eight years. After your child has attained the ability to understand symbols (by 18 to 24 months of age), you can use symbolic play to communicate with her about ongoing conflicts when they are not happening. Through a make-believe story, you can re-enact your conflict and make it humorous and silly so she laughs. For example, if your child repeatedly refuses to let you brush her teeth, you can create a tooth-brushing story with dolls, puppets, or stuffed animals (for example, a rabbit family). Play the parts of a mother rabbit and a baby rabbit who doesn't want to let the mother rabbit brush her teeth. You can turn the game into nonsense play by exaggerating the baby rabbit's protests and resistance.

You can also invite your child to play the role of the baby rabbit and turn it into a power-reversal game by playing the role of a mother rabbit who acts powerless and who pleads and begs. Be sure to use your child's laughter as a cue for your role-playing behavior. You may discover that your child provides clues about possible solutions to the conflict. For example, she may suggest that both the mother rabbit and the baby rabbit brush their teeth at the same time.

Eight to twelve years. As your children grow too old for symbolic play with dolls, puppets, or stuffed animals, you can propose a role-reversal scenario about your conflict. Ask your child to play the role of you, the parent, while you play the role of a rebellious and uncooperative child. This kind of activity, which is a form of power-reversal play, can lead to much laughter, and it will help resolve tensions and foster cooperation. You can continue to use this approach during the teenage years. You may even gain some insights into your own behavior when see how your child imitates you!

Some of the things that you want your children to do may not interfere with your own needs, and may not even be necessary for your children's health or safety. Examples include keeping their own room clean and brushing their hair. For these types of conflicts, it may be wise to back off and let your children experience the natural consequences. If you feel exhausted from years of trying to get your daughter to clean up her room, you can tell her that she's old enough to clean it up by herself. She may need to experience the frustration of not finding what she wants before she feels the need to clean it up. Meanwhile, if the mess bothers you, you can simply close the door to her room. If your daughter always balks when you ask her to brush her hair, it may be time to let her decide whether or not to brush it. The natural consequence in this case would be having tangled hair or hearing people make negative comments about her appearance. Although this is not a playful approach, it teaches your children to take responsibility for their own lives, and it allows you to focus on more important issues.

* * *

If you consider the issue of cooperation and compliance with long-term goals in mind, the first step is to "win" your children over with playful approaches so they willingly cooperate. For ongoing conflicts, you can bring up the conflicts in playful ways when they are *not* happening. Some kinds of play (for example, role reversal) can be effective even with teenagers. As your children grow older, you can also use more verbal discussions and conflict resolution. Remember to limit your efforts to genuine conflicts of needs while letting your children learn to take responsibility for their lives.

Playful activities for increasing children's willingness to cooperate (when there is no immediate conflict)

Use play to bring up an ongoing conflict when it is *not* happening:

• Birth to two years: Nondirective child-centered play or contingency play with the real objects involved in the conflict (ex: put the car seat in the living room), power-reversal games

• Two to eight years: Symbolic play with the conflict theme (ex: a tooth-brushing story), nonsense play, power-reversal games

• Eight to twelve years: Act out the conflict using role reversal and power-reversal games

Chapter 3

Setting Limits

SETTING LIMITS REPRESENTS a major part of discipline because we must place numerous restrictions on children's behavior. You cannot let your children do whatever they want. If you set limits lovingly and without the use of punishments or rewards, you will maintain a good relationship with your children, and they will be less likely to rebel later on.

Most limits fall into one of two categories: restrictions that are necessary for your child's own health and safety, and those that protect others or the environment. To keep your child safe, you might have rules such as "no running with sharp objects" and "no bicycle riding without a helmet." Rules for protection of others or the environment might include "no drawing on the walls," "no stepping on the flowers," and "no yelling when mom is talking on the telephone."

As with eliciting cooperation (see previous chapter), some kinds of playful activities can help you set an immediate limit, and others can help children better accept inevitable limits in the long run. The following two sections address each of these situations.

When you must set an immediate limit

When you must set an immediate limit, the three guidelines to keep in mind are: give explanations and reasons, look for the underlying need, and use a playful approach.

Give explanations and reasons. Children need and deserve explanations when we must restrict their behavior (just as they need explanations when we want them to cooperate). When they learn the reasons why we expect them to refrain from doing what they want to do, they will be more likely to abide by the rules and also remember them. Children frequently forget rules, so you can expect to give several reminders and explanations. Be aware, however, that you cannot expect children under the age of two to understand the concept of a rule. For children that young, you will need to make the limits part of your child's environment (such as baby-proofing your home) and provide constant supervision and redirection of your child's behavior.

Look for the underlying need. In addition to giving explanations, you can find ways to meet your child's underlying need. For example, if your child draws on the walls, explain to him that we don't draw on the walls, and offer him alternative places on which to draw. Tell him that he can draw on paper, use chalk on a chalk board, or paint at an easel, and provide him with the materials for these alternatives. Boredom can cause disagreeable behavior, so remember to bring toys, books, or games to places where you might have to wait, such as a doctor's office or post office. If your child has something to do, he will be less likely to do something annoying.

Use a playful approach. In addition to the first two guidelines, you can use playful activities to set a limit. The use of nonsense play can be especially effective for times when you need a quick way to "win" your child over to your side so that he will refrain from acting inappropriately. For example, you can pretend that your child is a machine, and say: "I guess I have to find the OFF button." You then proceed to press on different parts of his body (such as the top of his head or his nose), pretending to look for the magic button that will stop his behavior. Another approach is to assume the role of your child's favorite storybook villain while commanding him, with mock seriousness, to stop his behavior. For example, you can say in an evil tone of voice: "The wicked witch of the west commands you to stop throwing toys!"

A mother reported the following example illustrating a playful approach for setting a limit.

> One day, I was working in the garden planting some new baby plants. My three-year-old son was purposefully getting in the way and threatening to hurt the little plants. I asked him if he wanted to help me plant them, but he refused. I started to become very annoyed, but then I realized that he just wanted to get some of the attention that the plants were getting. So, I said, "Honey, you are my little baby cucumber plant, and I need to put you in the dirt so you can grow!" He happily agreed. I dug a big hole, put him in it, and covered him with dirt. I kissed him and doted on him the whole time, saying things like, "You are such a sweet little plant. I can't wait for you to grow big and make some yummy cucumbers!" Then I watered him and patted down the dirt. He loved every minute of it! After that, he let me finish planting the rest of the plants.

The effectiveness of playful approaches stems partly from the fact that they create a loving connection between you and your child. This need for connection may be the underlying reason that causes your child's obnoxious behavior in the first place.

Of course, there will be times when you must stop your child from doing something immediately, perhaps for his own safety, and you may not have time to find a playful solution. An obvious example would be if your child starts to run into the street. But even in situations where you need to act quickly and physically restrain your child, there is no need to punish him.

If your child's behavior is not dangerous, but merely annoying to other people, you may also need to set a firm limit. For example, if your child wants to push all the buttons in an elevator (making the ride last much longer than necessary by stopping at each floor), his behavior may be problematic, especially in the presence of other people. You will need to tell your child to stop pushing the buttons.

If he does not heed your verbal instructions and explanations, you may need to firmly (but lovingly) restrain his arms. Perhaps you can ride in an empty elevator with him another time and let him experiment with the buttons to satisfy his curiosity.

If your child persistently repeats aggressive or hurtful behavior, see Chapter 6 (Anger and aggression) for suggestions of playful ways to intervene. See also Part 3 to understand and resolve possible sources of stress or trauma that lie at the root of your child's behavior.

When you do not need to set an immediate limit

In addition to these tips for dealing with an immediate need to restrict your child's behavior, you can play power-reversal games in which your child gets to break rules while you pretend to be angry. This playful approach might not help in the short term (when you are actually trying to set a limit), but it can help in the long term. The effectiveness resides in the fact that these games give children an opportunity to release frustrations and feelings of powerlessness through laughter. After playing these games, children are often more willing to follow your rules and obey necessary restrictions.

The following three games provide opportunities for playful rule breaking: mother may I, animal cave game, and silly rules. These activities will be especially effective if your child laughs, so try to make them fun and silly. Each game is described below.

Mother may I. In the traditional version of this game, the children line up at the end of a room or yard while you stand alone at the other end. You then give instructions to one child at a time, telling him or her to move forward in a certain way. For example, you say: "Take three baby steps forward." Before your child can move, she must ask "mother, may I?", and you then reply "yes." If she forgets to ask permission, she is not allowed to move forward. You then give instructions to another child, and so on. Possible kinds of steps include baby steps, giant steps, twirly steps, sideways steps, jumping steps, and backward steps. You can play this game either competitively or cooperatively. If you play competitively, the first child to reach you is the winner. If you wish to play cooperatively, avoid mentioning winners or losers, and end the game with a group hug after all the children reach you. This game also works with just one adult and one child.

To make this game more fun and therapeutic, your children can try to sneak closer to you when they think you are not looking. You can find a pretext to look away or even leave for a short time. When you look at them again, be sure to feign surprise at how close they are getting to you by saying: "How did you get that close? I didn't tell you to move!" They will probably start to giggle and continue to sneak forward when they think you are not looking.

You can also reverse the roles. After your child understands the basic game, allow her to play the role of the mother (or father). Children greatly enjoy giving instructions and restrictions, especially to their own parents. Don't be surprised if your child gleefully replies "no" when you ask "mother, may I?" Your child will enjoy this game even more if you pretend to be upset and frustrated at these restrictions. To increase your child's enjoyment, fall on your knees and beg: "Please, mother. Let me take just *one* teeny tiny baby step."

Animal cave game. Games involving imaginary caves, nests, or cages can also help your children accept rules and restrictions. You can create an imaginary cave with a large hoop on the floor, a chalk circle on a sidewalk, or a circular rope. Tell your child that he is a baby lion who lives in a cave. You are the mother lion, and you must make sure that your little lion cub doesn't escape. Then put your child inside the circle and turn your back or walk a short distance away, saying: "I hope my cub stays in the cave. I'm going to hunt for some food." Most children will sneak out of the cave. When your child does this, you can show mock anger, chase your child, and put him back in the cave. Repeat the scene as often as your child wishes. You can also reverse the roles. The following example illustrates this game.

When my grandchildren were four and eight years old, I used a large plastic hoop to create an imaginary cave in our back yard, and I told them that I was a mama bear and they were my cubs. I instructed them to stay in the cave while I went to hunt for some food, and I said that there was a wolf lurking in the forest. After they understood that the goal of the game was to escape from the cave, they enjoyed sneaking out when they thought I wasn't looking. I pretended to be angry and told them sternly to keep all of their paws inside the cave. We then embellished the game by having one of them play the role of the wolf (with a wolf mask) while the other played the role of the cub. Then they wanted me to be the cub while one of them played the role of the mother bear and the other played the role of the wolf. I began to sneak out of the cave and let the mama bear push me back in. Then I snuck out again, pretending that I couldn't see the wolf, and let the wolf chase me and catch me. They laughed heartily during this activity.

Limits are often necessary to protect children from real dangers such as busy streets. In this game, the wolf provided a metaphor for all possible dangers in the world, which require the need for restricting children's behavior. So my grandchildren's laughter in this game may have indicated a release of fear in addition to a release of frustration about the need for limits and restrictions.

Silly rules. Games with silly rules are fun and therapeutic. They are especially useful if you have been authoritarian in the past but are trying to switch to a non-punitive approach to discipline. You can pretend to be an authoritarian parent who has a strict set of rules. During the game, you state one of your "rules" and your child tries to disobey you while you fake anger and make frantic attempts to stop her. Here are some examples of silly rules:

- You may not make any footprints on the ceiling.
- You are not allowed to eat with food in your mouth.
- You are not allowed to sleep on the piano.
- You must always brush your teeth before crossing the street.

- You must never, ever tell the truth.
- You may not eat the dog food.
- You may not put your toys away without my permission.
- You may not touch my little toe.

To illustrate the first rule, tell your child with mock seriousness: "You may not make any footprints on the ceiling." Your child then lies on her back with her legs in the air and tries to make footprints on the ceiling. You pretend to be angry while you try to "prevent" her from doing so. This activity will probably bring lots of hearty laughter.

Feel free to invent your own silly rules. In the following example, a mother reported the use of silly rules with her son.

My son (age five) loves to break rules, so I have learned to give him plenty of playful, convenient opportunities to do so. For example, I will say: "Don't you *dare* throw that pillow at me" or "I hope nobody steals this bowl of fruit salad while I am not looking." I am always careful to use a silly, playful voice so that he knows I am just pretending, and he gleefully transgresses. Because of this play, he doesn't feel the need to break my *real* rules as often.

Playful activities for setting limits

When you must set an immediate limit:
- Nonsense play in which you set a limit in a playful, silly way (ex: Pretend that your child is a machine and look for the "off" button)

When you do not need to set an immediate limit:
- Power-reversal games that allow your child to break rules while you pretend to be angry (ex: mother may I, animal cave game, silly rules)

Chapter 4

Toilet Training

MANY PARENTS EXPERIENCE problems with toilet training. If you use a traditional approach and wait until your child is at least two years old, toilet training can go very smoothly. Some parents avoid the use of diapers altogether by paying close attention to their baby's cues right from the start. However, problems can arise with either approach.

A child's resistance to using a toilet has many possible causes, one of which is the use of authoritarian discipline. If you try to control your child's behavior with punishments or rewards, she may rebel against your efforts to control her. You can solve the problem by switching to a non-authoritarian approach. Let your child take the lead and decide when she wants to wear underpants instead of diapers. Rather than create external rewards, try to build on her inherent desire to grow up and do things the way other children and adults do them. Don't dwell on successes and failures.

Children often resist using the toilet after traumatic events, such as starting a new school, the birth of a sibling, parental divorce, illness, hospitalization, or a death in the family. Children who experience these kinds of stresses or traumas may become toilet trained later than other children, or they may regress if they are already using a toilet before these events occur.

Some children become frightened by an event such as a toilet overflowing or a painful bowel movement. After these experiences, children sometimes refuse to use a toilet and may even become constipated because of a fear of defecating. A frightening event that is unrelated to defecating but that occurs when the child is sitting on the potty can also lead to resistance and constipation (for example, a clap of thunder).

If stress or trauma is the root cause of your child's resistance to use a toilet, you can help your child by using symbolic play with props and themes related to toileting. Therapists have found that free play with brown clay or play dough (to represent feces) can help children overcome constipation with psychological causes. Engage your child in play with a doll or stuffed animal, a child-sized potty, some doll-sized diapers and underpants, and some brown clay or play dough.

After you have provided the props and initiated the play theme, let your child take the lead from then on, but stay involved in the play. Your child will not be able to heal as effectively if you expect her to play by herself. The interactive nature of the play is a vital healing element, but there is no need to interpret your child's play.

If your child does not engage spontaneously in free play with the materials, you can suggest a play theme. Set the potty on the floor and tell your child that dolly (or teddy) has to pee or poop. (Use your own family's words for these biological functions.)

If you suspect that a fear of defecating lies at the root of your child's resistance, try to elicit laughter. For example, you can play the role of the doll by making it act fearful of the potty. You can even make the doll do outrageous things like urinating or defecating on a book or in a waste basket instead of in the potty. The goal is to engage your child and get her to laugh. The more she laughs during this kind of play, the quicker she will resolve the fears and tensions that are causing her to resist using a toilet. Here is an example from one of my clients.

Five-year-old Charlie used the toilet to urinate, but refused to defecate on either a toilet or a child-sized potty. Instead, he always requested a diaper when he needed to have a bowel movement. His parents had recently divorced after years of tension between them. Charlie spent half the week living with each parent. I told both parents to engage him in daily play sessions with a potty, a doll, and some brown play dough while encouraging laughter. Both parents followed my advice. One month later, the mother reported to me that her son had defecated on the potty and had said "that wasn't as hard as I thought it was going to be!"

Regression play can also help children who resist using the toilet after stressful or traumatic experiences. If your child agrees, put diapers on her and pretend that she is a baby. Rock her, feed her, sing to her, and play baby games such as peek-a-boo. This play should always be done in a spirit of loving acceptance, *never in a spirit of mockery or teasing*. When your child feels that she can regress to the safety of babyhood, and that you will not force her to act more grown up than she feels, she will gain the emotional strength necessary to move forward. Here's another example from one of my clients.

> Three-year-old Katie had regressed. She used to wear underpants and willingly use the potty. But lately, she had started requesting diapers again and refused to defecate anywhere but in a diaper. Her mother reported that Katie and both parents had experienced several serious illnesses. A younger sister was born when Katie was two-and-a-half years old. The mother had used punitive discipline with Katie because of exasperation and the exhaustion of dealing with two young children. I recommended both power-reversal games and regression games. Katie's regression in toileting indicated to me that she needed to regress to an earlier stage of development, unhampered by adult expectations to act older. Life had become very stressful for Katie and her family, and I felt that baby play would strengthen and nourish her. It would remind her of the time before her sister's birth when she and her mother had a loving connection. After the mother implemented my suggestions, Katie eventually began to use the toilet again.

The playful activities described in this chapter address some of the possible underlying causes of toileting problems. With this play-based approach, you may be able to avoid months of mutual frustration and power struggles.

Playful activities for toilet training problems

- Symbolic play with a doll, potty, and brown play dough

- Nonsense play (ex: have a doll urinate or defecate in inappropriate places)

- Regression games

Chapter 5

Use of "Bad" Language

AROUND THE AGE OF FOUR, many children start to use offensive language. They hear swear words and other expressions from their own parents or from other children, and they quickly discover that the words have enormous power to elicit strong reactions from other people. This reaction makes the words especially fun to say because the child feels immensely powerful. Children also tend to use rude words after someone else has spoken rudely to them. By repeating the words, they may be trying to work through the hurt they felt.

Swear words intrigue children because the words often refer to sexual activity or anatomy, as well as the functions of urinating and defecating. Children who have just recently learned to use a toilet are very aware of their body's "private parts." By age four, many children are curious about sexuality and reproduction. Furthermore, they pick up on other people's embarrassment about these topics.

You will probably not have much success if you verbally correct your child when he uses swear words. Your child might stop saying the words in your presence, but he will probably continue to use them in your absence. Later, these words may become entrenched in his speech, especially when he feels angry. If you punish your child for swearing, you may damage your relationship with him, lower his self-esteem, and cause him to rebel later on.

You will probably have more success with a playful approach. Laughter will allow your child to release the two major emotions that lie at the root of his need to say swear words: embarrassment and powerlessness.

Power-reversal games are especially effective for eliciting laughter and changing this kind of behavior. When your child uses a bad word, you can fall on the floor dramatically and say: "Oh my goodness. That's such a strong word, it knocked me over!" This activity resembles power-reversal pillow fights, except that the swear word plays the role of the pillow that "knocks" the adult down.

In the following example, a mother used a form of power-reversal play as an effective intervention when her son used offensive language.

My four-year-old son had been doing a lot of name calling to me after being called some names by older kids at his school. It was clearly not doing any good for me to say things like "that hurts my feelings" or "we don't call people names in our family." So one day when we were in a grocery store, I decided to try a playful approach. He started saying, "Mommy, you're a stupid idiot. You're a double idiot." I told him, "I'm going to eat those idiots," and I reached toward his mouth with my fingers like pinchers. I then pretended to eat the bad words and said, "Wow, those idiots taste yucky!" He howled with laughter. He continued calling me names for another minute or so, and I kept "eating" the bad words. Eventually, I pretended to throw up on him (a big laughter trigger for him). For the next couple of weeks, I kept "eating" his words, and before I even realized it, he had stopped calling me names. I was extremely pleased and surprised by the result!

You can also pretend to be stupid and wrongly accuse a teddy bear (or other stuffed animal) of saying the bad word while putting on a display of exaggerated anger at the animal. After your child uses a bad word, point an accusing finger at the teddy bear and say with mock anger: "*Who* said that? Teddy bear, did you say that bad word? I don't *ever* want to hear you say that word again!" When your child repeats the word, as he most certainly will, you can pretend to be even angrier with teddy bear. By this time, your child will probably be laughing gleefully.

You can also use nonsense play to elicit laughter by saying the words incorrectly or using exaggeration. The following example describes how I handled my son's use of bad words.

> When Nicky was four years old, he began to use offensive words that he had heard at school. I created silly expressions by transforming the bad words into less offensive ones. For example, when he said "you're a poo poo head," I replied, "you're a poppy head!" One of our family's favorite transformed swear words was "fuming asphalt." He always laughed at my silly transformations and eventually stopped using offensive language.

Another form of nonsense play is to exaggerate the behavior. You can spend time with your child shouting swear words together while laughing. In the following example, a mother describes how her daughter spontaneously initiated this kind of play after being scolded by her grandfather.

> When Heather was four years old, we were eating dinner at my parents' house, and she dropped her drink on the hardwood floor. She immediately shouted, "Shit!" I giggled a bit because I knew she had heard the word from me. My dad's mouth dropped open, and he said sharply, "Heather, we do not use that kind of language in this house!" My parents don't curse, and I was never allowed to say such words in their home. Heather paused, became very quiet, climbed into my lap, and began to cry. I explained to my dad that she was only repeating a word that she had heard me say. He apologized to my daughter and then told me that I should not be speaking that way in front of her, and not at all. I took Heather to another room so she could continue crying with my support. She felt hurt and confused by her grand-

father's sharp and scolding tone of voice, and she cried for about fifteen minutes. Later that evening, we were jumping on our trampoline, and every time she landed, she said "shit." When she looked at me to see my reaction, I smiled and let her know it was fine. Then she began to yell it louder and louder with every jump while laughing hysterically. Then she grabbed me and we started to jump together and yell "shit" while laughing. After about twenty minutes of this game, we sat on the trampoline and talked about curse words. I told her that I had no problem with her expressing herself with any word she chose. But I also told her that she needed to be aware of her surroundings because most people will be offended by swear words. She pondered this and then came up with the following plan. If we were in a place where she wanted to curse, and if it was inappropriate, she would whisper the bad word in my ear. It was an effective plan. She actually didn't do this too often, but when she did whisper a word in my ear, it was primarily in front of my dad (in a loving, funny way). In public places with lots of people, she sometimes did it to see if she could get me to laugh. Heather is twelve years old now and has rarely cursed in her life except when she wants to have a good laugh with me. Out of the blue, she will say a curse word when we are alone together, and we always laugh hysterically.

These approaches may appear counterproductive at first because they will temporarily encourage your child to repeat the bad words in your presence, but the temptation to use them in other contexts will decrease. He will start to use offensive language more as an invitation to play with you and less as a way to feel powerful, shock others, or express anger. The playfulness and laughter will diminish the tension or embarrassment connected with these words. Also, by helping your child release feelings of powerlessness, this play will reduce your child's need to seek power by swearing. Eventually, he will stop using these words altogether.

Playful activities for children
who use "bad" language

- Power-reversal games (ex: adult scolds a teddy bear, or the bad word knocks the adult down or makes the adult vomit)

- Nonsense play (ex: invent silly swear words, or repeat offensive words loudly together while laughing)

Chapter 6

Anger and Aggression

THIS CHAPTER DESCRIBES playful interventions that you can do with aggressive children. It's important to remember that the cause of aggressive behavior is usually some kind of stress or unhealed trauma, and that painful feelings always lie at the root of a child's aggression. A history of abuse, neglect, authoritarian discipline, frightening events, medical trauma, or aggression from other children can cause children to hit, bite, or bully other children. In Part 3, you will find tips for addressing specific sources of stress or trauma.

The following examples from my clients illustrate aggressive behavior in young children following stress or trauma (or during stressful times).

- A 15-month-old girl began to pull her mother's hair after watching the terrorist attacks on TV on 9–11.

- A two-year-old boy acted very aggressively toward other children. He had a history of multiple medical interventions, beginning with a traumatic birth. He had been hospitalized as an infant and had been to the emergency room three more times during his second year for food poisoning and other illnesses.

- A three-year-old boy began to bite other children at school after his parents started talking about getting a divorce (even though they had never mentioned this to him).

- A four-year-old boy frequently spit at his parents. His mother had been diagnosed with breast cancer when he was nine months old and had undergone three years of treatments (including several surgeries and chemotherapy).

- An eleven-year-old girl became aggressive at home as the date approached for her to start attending a new school.

Some aggressive children have no history of major trauma but simply an accumulation of daily frustrations, disappointments, overstimulation, or unmet needs. So even in the absence of obvious stress or trauma, aggressive behavior can occur if the children have not had opportunities to heal from these daily stresses.

Instead of punishing children for aggressive behavior or lecturing them on the virtues of kindness, look for ways to help them release painful emotions harmlessly. Several kinds of play-based activities can reduce a child's aggression.

Research has shown that aggressive children benefit from nondirective child-centered play. If your child acts aggressively, try to find the time to engage her in weekly play sessions with you in a room with a variety of toys, such as blocks, dolls, small figures, animals, and vehicles. Daily play sessions would produce even quicker results. Be sure to let her take the initiative while you show empathy and acceptance. If she wants you to join her more actively, do whatever she tells you to do, but let her continue to direct the play. By providing regular child-centered play sessions, you will strengthen your bond with your child, and she will gain a sense of trust and safety. When she feels safe enough, she will use the play sessions to express emotions resulting from stress or trauma. With your love and acceptance of these emotions, she will be able to work through her feelings and problems.

Power-reversal games are also useful for aggressive children because they provide a safe, healthy outlet for aggression and allow tension-release through laughter. An effective power-reversal game is one in which you pretend to be weak, powerless, ignorant, frightened, or stupid. This form of play has many variations. Children often initiate power-reversal play when they feel angry. A father reported the following example:

> My six-year-old boy squished a piece of paper into a ball and threw it at me while saying, "Watch out, it's a bomb!" I put on a mock display of fear and pretended to die dramatically, which brought peals of laughter from him.

If your child really tries to hurt you, you can channel his aggressive energy into a power-reversal game. Here's an example of the use of power-reversal play with an angry child.

> I was staying with a family during one of my workshop tours. One day, the mother (Helen) and I were sitting at her kitchen table, and Helen told me that they had moved four times since her son was born. "We've just moved into this house, and we love it here," she said. Her four-year-old son, Matthew, was standing quietly nearby, listening to our conversation. Suddenly, he walked over to Helen and hit her on the upper arm as hard as he could. She looked at me, baffled by her son's behavior (because he had never hit her before), and asked, "What should I do?" I turned to Matthew and asked him if he was mad at his mommy. He replied emphatically, "Yes!" I then asked him if he was mad at her for making him move from his old home. He replied with another, very definite, "Yes!" I then asked him, "Would you like to have a pillow fight with your mommy?" Enthusiastically, he replied, "YES!" and eagerly fetched an armful of pillows from a bedroom. We moved into the living room, where Helen engaged him in a pillow fight. I encouraged her to fall on the floor every time he hit her with a pillow. Matthew loved the game and laughed uproariously every time his mother "fell" on the floor. At one point, he set a pillow down on the carpet and told her, "Here, mommy. Here's

a pillow so you won't crack your head open when you fall down." He then proceeded to whack her some more with the pillow while laughing gleefully. After twenty minutes of this play, Matthew felt much better and did not hit his mother during the next two days of my visit. According to Helen's follow-up report to me, Matthew hit her again about a week later, and she suggested that they have another pillow fight. He again laughed heartily while hitting his mother with pillows. Then, about a week or two after that, he said, "Mom, I'm angry, let's have a pillow fight." After that, he never hit his mother again, but they had lots of pillow fights!

I later explained to Helen that young children often blame their parents for anything in their lives that they don't like even though it might not be the parents' fault. Also, it's hard for children to feel safe expressing anger about something that obviously pleases their parents (such as a move to a new home).

Power-reversal play with older children (and even teenagers) can take the form of a wrestling match, as the following example of my daughter illustrates.

When Sarah was twelve years old, she sometimes felt stressed after school and directed her anger at me. Although she never hit me, she sometimes yelled at me. At those times, I invited her to wrestle with me. We would stand facing each other, clasp hands with outstretched arms, and try to push each other across the room while making angry faces and growling at each other. I would resist at first but eventually give in and let her push me onto the couch. As she grew older and stronger, I no longer had to fake weakness, because she easily pushed me onto the couch! She always laughed during these wrestling matches and often wanted to cuddle with me afterwards. This play allowed her to express her anger, release tensions through laughter, and re-establish a loving bond with me.

Some parents feel uncomfortable with this approach for handling their children's aggressive behavior. They worry that if they encourage children to hit or push the parents, the children will be more likely to continue doing so in the future. However, this outcome does not usually occur. When children hit or push their parents playfully while laughing, this actually *reduces* their aggressive tendency.

Be aware that little children may need information about what is hurtful and what is not. Also, children approaching adolescence may need feedback about their own developing strength because they may not realize how strong they are. It may be necessary to set ground rules during active power-reversal play so that nobody gets hurt. For example, you may want to include rules about not hitting each other's faces or stopping the play immediately when the other person says "stop."

By accepting your children's angry feelings, you will teach them that your connection with them is stronger than their anger and that nothing can destroy the loving bond between you. If you respond punitively to your child's aggressive behavior, she may learn to suppress her angry feelings, but this will occur at a huge cost to her emotional health and her relationship with you. Suppressed anger can lie at the root of later substance abuse, violence, depression, or anorexia.

Nonsense play provides another approach for dealing with children's anger. A mother described to me how she used a version of nonsense play (silly exaggeration of feelings) with a group of angry children while volunteering at her daughter's school.

I volunteer at my daughter's nursery school (with three- to five-year-olds). One day, I noticed a lot of pushing and other forms of aggression, which I hadn't seen for a while. That day, the children at my snack table were spilling things and blaming each other, and it was really disagreeable. So we sat in a big circle, and we all practiced making angry faces. I called the feelings "strong feelings" rather than labeling them as bad or mean. I said, "I see a lot of strong feelings. Can you make some strong, angry faces?" The children really got into that. I clarified, "No sounds, just faces." We went around the circle and looked at each child's angry face. They imitated the boy, Max, from the book, *Where the Wild Things Are* (by Maurice Sendak). One child rolled his terrible eyes, and another showed her terrible claws, just like in the book. Then we made some happy faces. The kids loved this activity and laughed a lot. Then they all started playing well together. I felt very good about this approach because it really worked.

Some children become aggressive in a group setting after they have been hit or pushed by other children. This experience leaves them feeling unsafe. They may then over-react when they feel that another child has invaded their personal space. If you know the underlying cause of your child's aggression, you can engage her in symbolic play with props and themes relating to the original stress or trauma. Here is an example of a three-year-old child whose parents brought him for parent-child play coaching.

Three-year-old Xavier began pushing other children at school after he himself had been pushed. His teacher used the concept of work areas, which were small rugs where children could sit to play with the materials. Children were not supposed to bother other children who were sitting in their work areas. To re-create the atmosphere at his school, I set some little bears on a square piece of cloth and told Xavier it was the bears' work area. He eagerly joined in the play. After a while, he pulled a little train around but almost cried when the train bumped into the little bears. I reflected his feelings by asking, "Did the little bears get scared when the train came so close?" He replied, "Yes." After that, he was very careful to pull the train *around* the bears. At the end of the session, he wanted to take the train home with him. When I said that he couldn't take it, he started crying and had a good cry in his parents' arms as they carried him out the door. A month later, his parents brought him again for a play session. He immediately recreated the same scene as before, by putting the little bears on their work area. Then he again started pulling the train around. This time, however, he found a solution by placing the bears on a nearby table so the train could pass by without bumping into them.

This example shows that children eagerly engage in play that symbolizes issues of concern to them. Through play, they can find creative solutions. In this example, the train may have symbolized the rough children at the child's school. His idea of moving the bears to the table may have helped him remember to play farther away from the rough children when he wanted to feel safe. This example also shows that this kind of play can bring up deep feelings and lead to crying. The fact that I did not let him take the train home with him gave him a pretext to start crying, but it was probably not the real issue that he was crying about. His tears may have helped him release some of the stress from his school experience. When children cry during or after a play session, I consider the crying to be a healthy release, just like laughter.

The following example further illustrates the use of both power-reversal play and symbolic play with a child who had a lot of pent-up anger.

A mother brought her four-year-old son, Fred, for a parent-child play session because of his aggressive behavior. Fred had a six-year-old sister who needed a lot of attention because of a medical disability. The mother felt that Fred's difficult behaviors, in addition to her daughter's needs, had weakened her emotional connection with him. This further contributed to his feelings of insecurity and anger. She was especially disturbed when he told her things like: "I'm going to chop you up. I'm going to live with a different family. You're a bad mom." I began the play session by engaging Fred in power-reversal play in which he frightened his mother with plastic spiders, snakes, and monster puppets while laughing heartily. Whenever his mother fell onto the

couch, Fred fell on her in an awkward attempt to get close.
I encouraged her to give him a loving hug each time he fell
on her. Then I used a bear family as props to tell a story
about a brother bear wanting something that belonged to
his sister. Fred eagerly participated in the story and announced that the brother bear was *older* than the sister bear.
Then he took the brother bear and pretended that it was a
bee flying around. With much glee, he made it attack and
sting the other bear family members.

In a follow-up session with the mother four days later, she felt that
the play session had strengthened her connection with her son and
helped reduce his aggressive behavior. She planned to continue the
play at home.

This example brings up an important point. The child wanted
to connect physically with his mother, and he showed this desire
by falling on her. When children seek closeness but also have a lot
of anger, their attempts to connect may include aggressive behavior
such as hitting, pushing, or falling on their parents. These children
usually need some active power-reversal play to release anger before
they feel ready to connect in gentler ways.

Many parents ask me about war play, wondering if they should
let their children play with guns and other weapons. Children often
initiate war play as soon as they hear about violence and war, either
through books, TV, films, or the Internet. Children who have a parent or other relative in the armed forces will probably show a great
interest in war play. Little boys identify more with war play than
girls because most of the media images on this topic portray men
rather than women. Even boys who never watch these various media
eventually learn about wars and violence. When they do, they often
feel curious, frightened, and confused. One way that they attempt
to process these various emotions and assimilate the information is
through play that mimics what they have seen or heard.

There is no need to give your children toy guns or other weapons. But even if your son has no toy weapons at home, he will prob-

ably create his own with sticks or toys. Children have such a strong need to engage in war play that it is not very effective to ban this kind of play unless they are hurting each other.

Instead of trying to forbid war play, you can help your child process emotions by turning his play into a power-reversal game. If your little boy points his fingers at you, and says "bang, bang, you're dead," the most helpful response is for you to pretend to die as dramatically as possible. The goal is to encourage your son to laugh and to keep him laughing as long as possible. This laughter will help him reduce anxiety and tension. Furthermore, your playful attitude will let him know that you are not afraid of his aggression, thereby reassuring him that there is room in your relationship for all kinds of feelings, even the most frightening ones. This playful response of yours will *not* encourage your son to become aggressive or hurtful toward others. Instead, it will probably reduce his aggressive urges.

Playful activities for aggressive behavior

• Nondirective child-centered play

• Active power-reversal games (ex: pillow fight)

• Nonsense play (ex: silly exaggeration of anger)

• Symbolic play with a theme relating to stressful events at the root of the child's aggression

---

Chapter 7 _____

Sibling Rivalry

THIS CHAPTER PROVIDES playful suggestions for dealing with sibling rivalry, which ranks high on the list of parenting challenges. In Part 3, you will find suggestions for helping children cope with the birth of a sibling, which can be a major stressful event. Jealousy can occur immediately after the sibling's birth or later on when your younger child starts to interfere with her older sibling's play or openly compete with him for your attention.

I recommend finding the time to play with each of your children individually, using nondirective child-centered play. Provide building materials, dolls, small vehicles, and art materials, and then give your child your full, undivided attention while letting her take the lead. Be sure to do whatever she requests during these special play times. Perhaps she wants you to play store with her or simply watch her build with blocks.

Half an hour per day of this kind of play with each child would be ideal. If you cannot set aside that much time with each child, then do whatever you can. Even as little as half an hour, once a week, can help a child feel loved and special. Make arrangements for your other children so you are free to focus entirely on one child at a time. I recommend that you refrain from answering the telephone during these special play times. You could even set a timer and let your child know that you will play with her until it rings.

Some parents enjoy taking their children individually out to lunch, shopping, or to a movie. Although these activities are fun, they may not meet your child's need for one-on-one attention as successfully as simply playing with her at home. If you let your child choose how to spend the special time with you, she may surprise you by wanting to stay home and play with you.

There are two benefits of these nondirective play sessions. The first is that your undivided attention will help your child feel validated and loved, thereby counteracting her feelings of sibling jealousy. The second benefit is that your child may use your attention during the play to express feelings. The following incident occurred during one of my parent-child play coaching sessions:

> Four-year-old Maria was extremely jealous of her three-year-old brother, and the children often fought with each other. During the session with Maria and her mother, Maria chose to play with small plastic toys representing people and animals. As her mother and I paid attention to her, she set up a family scene with two children: a girl and a baby. She put the baby figure on the other side of the room with a cow while the girl figure engaged in activities with both the mother and father figures. When I asked her to tell us about her play, she explained, "The baby is over there, and he has a cow to give him milk. The little girl is playing with her mommy and daddy." I asked, "Does the little girl want the baby to be part of the family?" She replied, "He doesn't really need a mother, because he has a cow."

Through her play, Maria expressed her wish to have her parents all to herself. Her mother and I acknowledged this wish by accepting her symbolic family scene. Children enjoy this kind of play because it allows them to express their emotions and feel accepted. You can encourage symbolic play by providing a doll family or teddy bear family that reflects your own family. You do not need to verbally interpret the underlying meaning. Your attention and acknowledgment of your child's play are sufficient.

If your child acts aggressively toward a younger sibling, you will need to stop the behavior to protect the younger child. You can accomplish this by suggesting a power-reversal game in which you invite your older child to direct her aggression toward *you* instead of her sibling. If this suggestion does not stop the aggressive behavior, you may need to stop the child firmly, but lovingly, to protect the other child. Then repeat your invitation for a power-reversal game.

The following example from one of my clients illustrates the use of power-reversal play with a jealous child.

> Three-year-old Gwen had become increasingly angry and aggressive. She frequently mistreated her baby brother (seven months old). She would become rough or overly intrusive with him, or she would force him to do things that he didn't want to do. During a telephone consultation with Gwen's mother, one of my suggestions was for her to play power-reversal games with Gwen, for example, a pillow fight in which she should let Gwen knock her down. I told the mother to fall dramatically onto the floor and encourage as much laughter as possible. Two weeks later, she sent me a follow-up report by e-mail, "The pillow fighting has worked wonders!"

Another mother describes her use of power-reversal play with her jealous three-year-old daughter in the following example.

> Melissa was only two years old when Aline was born. Right from the start, she tried to pinch her, pull her arm off, or push her off the bed. Now, at age three, she is still very jealous of her sister and still tries to hurt her frequently. I've started using a playful approach. I let her push me down, pull me up, and roll me over. That's one of the games we play a lot whenever we can. She calls it "fall you down." And I let her tickle me, too. She really enjoys these games and laughs hard, and she always treats her sister better after playing them.

For chronic sibling rivalry, you can also play power-reversal games in which *both* children try to knock you down with pillows. Of course, you must pretend to be weak and frightened while letting them overpower you. If these activities bring laughter, then you are on the right track. A mother described the following power-reversal game between her two sons and their father.

> When my sons were between two and six years of age, they loved to push their father off the couch when he was lying on it. Of course, we put pillows on the floor to soften his fall. The two boys worked as a team in order to successfully dislodge him so they could have the couch to themselves. The boys and their dad all laughed heartily during this game. The boys felt strong and powerful whenever they managed to make their father fall off. This game helped the boys bond with each other through mutual collaboration while enjoying magical moments with their father.

When your children fight over a toy, you have a choice of two possible responses (other than separation or punishment, which I don't recommend). You can either do mediation with the children or engage them in specific forms of play. The mediation approach begins by removing the toy temporarily to stop the conflict and then inviting each child to tell his or her version and express emotions. After reflecting back each child's feelings, you can then encourage the children to think of their own solution to the problem while you refrain from taking sides or imposing your own ideas. Children often come up with highly creative and original solutions to their conflicts. However, very young children may need the adult mediator to suggest possible solutions, such as taking turns, sharing, or playing with something else.

Children's different developmental levels can make it hard to find a solution through mediation. For example, young children have a difficult time with deferred gratification (such as waiting for their turn), as well as understanding another person's point of view. Their behavior can seem stubborn and egocentric because of these cognitive limitations. But even though the mediation approach described above may not always work immediately with young children, it can help children attain these important developmental milestones while learning conflict-resolution skills.

A playful approach is especially effective for children who are too young to grasp these concepts and also in situations where the children's intense emotions interfere with their ability to think clearly enough for mediation. A version of power-reversal play usually works well in this situation. Grab the toy and run away with it while inviting the children to cooperate with each other to retrieve it. As they chase you together, they will temporarily be on the same "team." You can then slow down or pretend to stumble and let them catch you to retrieve the toy. If you don't have the energy or space to run, you can hide the toy in a visible place and explain that you have put it away. Then you show mock surprise when they find it. Or you can let the children hide the toy together, and then you make feeble efforts to look for it while pretending that you cannot find it.

With these playful activities, the children's anger and competitive feelings will soon dissolve as they switch to a cooperative activity in which they are on the same side as their siblings. This approach can turn a potential battle into an enjoyable game, and the laughter will reduce frustration. After these games, the children will be less likely to fight over the toy.

Nonsense play can also be effective in some situations of sibling rivalry. You can help everybody release tensions through laughter by playfully exaggerating the dynamics involved. The following experience with my own children illustrates this approach.

Nicky (age eleven) and Sarah (age six) were fighting. Finally, Sarah kicked Nicky so hard that he complained to me. We had the following dialog:

Me: What's going on?
Nicky: She kicked me.
Sarah: He wouldn't let me have the toy.
Nicky: She didn't share her candy yesterday in the car.
Sarah: He didn't let me sit in the front seat when it was my turn.

Me (to Nicky): What would you like to do to Sarah now, to pay her back?

Nicky: I'd like to sit on her (laughs while pretending to sit on his sister).

Me (to Sarah): Sarah, it's your turn now. What would you like to do to Nicky? We can't let this stop. You've got to pay him back.

Sarah: I want to hit him on the head (laughs while pretending to hit her brother).

They continued playfully to plan how they would "pay each other back," and ended up having great fun while laughing heartily. After that, they played happily together.

A father reported the following incident, which further illustrates the use of playful exaggeration (nonsense play) in helping children resolve conflicts with each other.

We were sitting at the table (six of us) and our four-year-old twins both wanted the same chair, yelling "go away" to each other. Both were stubborn and on the verge of tears. I said, "Let's all say 'go away' to the person on our right." So all six of us did so, and the children started laughing. Then we said "go away" to the person on our left. Then we started telling imaginary people under the table and on the roof to go away. After much laughter and silliness, one of the twins simply moved to another chair, which resolved the problem. I never suggested this move or mentioned the chair at all. He moved of his own accord.

In the example above, the children's laughter allowed them to release frustration and anger, which reduced their need to compete with each other for the same chair.

Cooperative activities can also reduce competition among siblings. Build a cooperative tower with blocks, tell a cooperative story, make music, bake cookies, or work on art projects together. Many children enjoy cooperative doctor play with mom or dad playing the role of a patient while the children play the role of nurses or doctors. The nature of this activity requires that your children cooperate to take care of you.

You can also adapt traditional sports or games so that nobody wins or loses. If you play a competitive game with your children, such as tennis or chess, try to emphasize having fun together and improving individual skills while minimizing the importance of winning. You can even give yourself a handicap, for example, play tennis with your left hand (if you are right-handed) or play chess without your queen. When you build up your children's confidence in their own abilities, they won't feel the need to compete as fiercely with their siblings or other children. Here's an observation of my grandchildren.

> I watched my seven-year-old grandson teach his little sister to play checkers. At three years of age, she was a bit young to learn the game, but he patiently repeated the rules while showing her how to move her pieces. He did not play his best and even allowed her to acquire a king before he did. When I commented favorably on this to his father (my son), he said, "He's imitating the way I'm teaching him to play chess. I don't use my queen and I often let him win." Because of this supportive learning experience with his father, my grandson did not feel the need to compete with his sister or show his superiority by beating her in a game.

If you have difficulty implementing these various activities for coping with sibling rivalry, it's probably because you lacked role models for this kind of parenting. Perhaps your first impulse is to yell or use punishment when your children fight with each other, because that's what your own parents did to you. However, if you can manage to shift to a playful approach once in a while, you will address the underlying problem much more effectively than with the use of harsh words or punishment. The laughter during these activities will help dissolve the painful emotions that underlie sibling rivalry, including frustration, anger, insecurity, anxiety, and powerlessness. These games will also strengthen your connection to your children while bringing joy to your family.

Playful activities for sibling rivalry

- Nondirective child-centered play with each individual child

- Symbolic play with dolls or an animal family

- Power-reversal games with each individual child and also with both children on the same "side" against you

- Nonsense play with silly exaggeration of the rivalry dynamics

- Cooperative games and activities

Chapter 8

Lying, Cheating, and Stealing

WHEN CHILDREN lie, cheat, or steal, parents naturally worry and wonder what to do. Several possible causes account for these behaviors.

Some lying represents wishful thinking. When a young child tells a story about riding a horse at a friend's house, even though you know he did not ride a horse, you can simply accept his statement and ask him how he liked it. There is no need to accuse him of lying. You can also acknowledge the underlying wish by saying, for example: "Do you wish you had a horse?"

If your child is obviously inventing an imaginary story, you can say: "That sounds like a lovely story. Shall we write it down?" Then invite him to dictate it to you and illustrate it. Much of human creativity originates in wishful thinking, so you don't want to stifle your child's imagination.

The use of punitive discipline can lead to lying, cheating, and stealing because punishment inevitably causes anxiety, insecurity, and a desire for revenge. Children whose parents use punitive consequences will naturally tend to lie when they think that they can avoid being "caught." It's much easier for a child to say "those crumbs on the rug are not mine" than to face painful consequences. In addition, frequently punished children may try to feel better and boost their self-esteem by cheating during a game or taking something they want. They then lie about their behavior because they fear punitive consequences.

If your children show any of these antisocial behaviors, the first step is to switch to a non-authoritarian approach to discipline. These behaviors do not necessarily indicate that your children will grow up to be delinquents. However, if you continue to use punitive discipline, their antisocial behavior may increase with age.

It's important to realize that even children raised with non-punitive discipline may occasionally deny a direct accusation of wrongdoing if they think they did nothing wrong. For example, if you discover that your daughter gave some of her personal medicine to another child, it's best to avoid a direct question ("Did you give some of your medicine to a friend?"), especially if you already know the truth. Your daughter may say "no" in an attempt to deny the accusation of wrongdoing inherent in your tone of voice. A better approach would be to tell your daughter what you learned, ask her if she was trying to help her friend feel better, and then give her information about the risks of sharing medicine. You can give this information while validating her desire to help her friend.

Lying, cheating, and stealing can also be symptoms of deeper problems, such as difficult sibling or peer relationships. For example, a child whose friends or siblings have teased, criticized, or bullied him may cheat or steal in a misguided attempt to regain a sense of confidence and self-worth. If a child's siblings or friends always win games or excel in other ways, or if he himself has some kind of handicap, he may suffer from low self-esteem and begin to cheat in an effort to compete with the other children. On the other hand, a child with an ill or handicapped brother or sister may feel insecure and unloved because of all the special care and attention that his sibling receives. Feelings of insecurity can also arise following the birth of a sibling, parental divorce, parental illness, or other family stress. So if your child begins to cheat or steal, even though you use a non-punitive approach to discipline, it's possible that he is suffering from difficult peer or sibling relationships or other forms of stress.

In these cases, cheating and stealing are symbolic but inappropriate ways for children to get their needs met and feel better about themselves. When a child wins a game, he momentarily experiences a boost of confidence and pride. Taking an object that belongs to someone else helps an emotionally deprived child feel that he has obtained something of worth. These inappropriate behaviors allow children to compensate symbolically for the factors that are missing in their lives or to cope with the chronic stress they are experiencing.

You may feel tempted to take a firm stand when your child cheats during a game or steals something. But correcting your child with harsh words or punishment will not work, because these consequences fail to address the underlying reasons for the child's behavior. In fact, they risk causing the child to feel even worse and may lead to more antisocial behavior later on.

A playful approach that addresses the cheating will be more effective in the long run than correcting your child. If your child creates kings for himself during a game of checkers when he thinks that you are not looking, you may want to end the game or insist on playing the correct way. A more helpful approach, however, is to realize that your child is inviting you to play a *different kind of game*. He is not really interested in playing a normal game of checkers at that moment. He wants to play a therapeutic game that will help him release emotions, gain confidence, deal with past failures, and feel better about himself.

You can acknowledge and accept your child's cheating behavior by saying: "I see that you are changing the rules. Do I get to have some kings too?" If he replies "no," then you can turn the activity into a power-reversal game by obeying his rules but pretending to be upset when he starts to win. ("Oh no, I'm losing!") The goal is to bring the cheating out in the open and encourage your child to laugh. You can play the role of a frustrated player and a "bad" loser, thereby mirroring how your child feels when *he* loses a game. The following example illustrates a playful response to a child's cheating behavior.

> I played a board game with a four-year-old child. The game involved a spinner that indicated the number of squares to move our pieces forward. The first to reach the end of the board was the winner. She had never played the game before, so I taught it to her. We played the game once through,

and my piece reached the end before hers. She didn't like this outcome although I had not referred to winning or losing. When we played a second time, she spun the spinner for her turns but stopped the arrow each time so it pointed to a number that she wanted. I pretended to be surprised and exclaimed, "How do you manage always to keep ahead of me?" She started giggling. When her piece reached the end of the board before mine, she placed it on the ending square with great glee. I pretended to cry and said, "I never caught up with you, boo hoo." She laughed heartily.

This role playing with exaggeration of emotions will allow your child to release tensions through laughter. It lets him know that you are willing to help him with difficult feelings of competition, inferiority, or insecurity. By joining your child in the *real* game that he needs to play at that moment, you will help him work through these painful emotions, and this will boost his self-confidence and make him *less* likely to cheat in the future. Furthermore, it will provide both of you with an enjoyable activity while strengthening your connection. The game that you end up playing may have nothing in common with the official game rules!

When children change game rules, it's important to take their age into account before assuming that they feel insecure or have low self-esteem. Young children do not have the same concept of rules as older children. The four-year-old girl in the example above quickly learned the rules of the game but did not see anything wrong with changing them to meet her wishes. For her, it was all part of the game. After the age of six or seven, children understand better that game rules should be respected. The same behavior in a ten-year-old child would therefore be a little more worrisome, especially if he tried to cheat secretly. But playful interventions based on power reversal can be effective for children of all ages.

You may find it more challenging to deal with stealing. If your child steals something from you, you can interpret that behavior as a plea for help with unmet needs, low self-esteem, insecurity, or pent-up anger. Try to probe beneath the surface to discover the underlying reason. If your child secretly takes money from your purse or eats one of your birthday chocolates without permission, the first step is to acknowledge the child's feelings ("You really wanted that chocolate"), but to understand that the money or chocolate represent deeper needs.

If your child takes something that belongs to someone else, you will need to insist that he return the stolen item. Try to find a way to do this lovingly while explaining the other person's feelings. Depending on the age of your child, you can gently probe beneath the surface. ("Do you wish that Dennis would play more with you?" "Do you wish that you had a toy like the one you took from him?" "Has he been mean to you?" "Does he have more friends than you?" and so on.) Then discuss (or role play) with your child more appropriate ways to get his needs met.

A playful approach can be effective, especially if your child denies that he stole something (either from you or from someone else). Don't force him to confess. Instead, accuse a stuffed animal: "Teddy bear, did you take that chocolate?" Then scold the teddy bear with fake seriousness: "Teddy bear, you mustn't take things that belong to other people!" By this time, your child will probably start to giggle. You can continue the playful activity by making the teddy bear "steal" additional items while you fake anger. You can even create a story in which a child bear steals items from a mother bear and builds a huge pile of stolen items in the middle of the room. The mother bear frantically searches for the stolen items even though they are in plain sight. Encourage your child to play one of the parts.

By incorporating the theme of stealing and lying into symbolic play with stuffed animals, you will help your child work through the underlying feelings. The playful exaggeration and silliness will bring therapeutic laughter and dissolve your child's feelings of anxiety and insecurity. In addition, your child may incorporate themes into the play that reveal his deeper motives or needs, thereby helping you understand him better.

Children who lie, cheat, or steal may also benefit from cooperative games and activities in which there are no winners or losers.

Together, you can invent cooperative versions of your favorite board games or sports. Your child will learn to relax and enjoy playing games without the pressure of competition.

I have played many cooperative group games with children between the ages of six and twelve. During these activities, I have noticed that children with low self-esteem and behavior problems tend to compare themselves with others even though the games are non-competitive. They typically say things such as "my team was better" or "I won." When I calmly explain that it's not a competition and that there are no winners or losers, these children usually relax and end up enjoying the games immensely.

Remember that children who lie, cheat, or steal are usually harboring painful emotions. The use of verbal correction or punishment will not help and may only worsen the situation. Children will benefit much more from interventions that allow them to resolve the underlying feelings. Through playful activities with these themes, you will help your children work through feelings of insecurity while building their self-confidence and strengthening their connection to you.

Playful activities for lying, cheating, and stealing

- Power-reversal games when your child cheats or changes the rules

- Symbolic play/nonsense play in which you role play activities about lying or stealing with stuffed animals, using exaggeration and silliness

- Cooperative games and activities

Chapter 9

Homework

HOMEWORK CAN CAUSE considerable stress for parents and children. Research has shown that homework is not necessary and that too much homework can actually be counterproductive while robbing children of important play time. Unfortunately, most schools give children homework assignments.

Many children find homework boring or disagreeable, and parents feel they must set and enforce homework rules. This situation can lead to a vicious cycle as children become increasingly resistant, and parents become increasingly authoritarian. The resulting power struggles can lead to mutual frustration and anger.

Your job is not to *make* your children do their homework but to help and support them. If you can think of yourself less as a dictator and more as a facilitator, things will probably go more smoothly. The following three mistakes can lead to homework struggles and conflicts: expecting children to complete their homework too soon after school, expecting children to do their homework alone, and treating the topic of homework too seriously.

After a full day of school and after-school activities, children need time to relax, play, and release stress from the day. If you allow your children to do so, they will be able to focus much better on their homework afterwards.

Most children don't like to do homework alone. I recommend offering to help with homework. Be aware, however, that your children may resist unbidden teaching, so don't give information or point out mistakes without their permission. Your children will probably benefit more from your explanations if you wait for their questions than if you offer unbidden information.

Homework doesn't have to be serious. Remember that children learn best through play. If you think of your children's homework as a wonderful opportunity for play and connection, you and your children will both enjoy it, and they will learn more quickly and effectively.

Some parents fear that a playful approach to homework will somehow "spoil" their children. They think that it's good for children to do things they don't want to do (such as tedious homework), because this will help them become successful and develop a good work ethic for later in life. This assumption is incorrect. Drudgery and hard work do not build character or lead to meaningful learning or good habits. Instead, they can lead to feelings that interfere with the learning process, such as resentment, anger, frustration, or boredom. Furthermore, forcing your children to do homework can damage your relationship with them.

Children are born highly motivated to develop their skills and strive for mastery. If the learning process were tedious and disagreeable, children would never learn to walk or talk. These tasks are difficult to master, yet children tackle them with obvious pleasure. Sometimes they become frustrated in their efforts to learn these skills, but they persevere with strong determination even though nobody tells them to do so. That's because the *process* of learning to talk or walk is naturally pleasurable for young children. They are highly motivated to learn these skills and don't need any kind of external control, punishments, or rewards to do so.

People of all ages learn best when they can follow their own interests. If your children show interest in dinosaurs, castles, rocks, or secret codes, they will probably enjoy books about these topics. They will also eagerly engage in activities relating to these interests, such as forming collections, creating, or building. Through these playful activities, they will learn effortlessly and joyfully about prehistoric times, the Middle Ages, geology, or cryptography.

One reason why children resist homework is that they have not chosen to learn those particular topics at that specific time or in that specific way. You can help your children, not by forcing them to do their homework, but by finding ways to make homework fun and by building on your children's own interests. Below are some examples of playful approaches to homework.

If your child has a hard time getting started with a reading assignment for a work of fiction, you can take turns reading different roles (using funny voices), or you can encourage your child to predict how the story will end. After reading the book, you and your child can act out the story with costumes and props or think of alternative endings.

For math assignments, it is always effective to work with concrete materials or real-life examples. These will make math more fun and also help your child grasp the underlying concepts. If your child struggles with a written math problem, you can change the example into one involving toys or objects that she is interested in, such as plastic dinosaurs, small toy cars, or cookies. If possible, provide real objects for your child to work with and turn the problem into a story or game.

A father reported the following experience.

> I was helping my twelve-year-old daughter with a math assignment involving ratios. The example in her homework was about the ratio of black keys to white keys on a piano. She had a difficult time grasping the concept and had no interest in pianos. But when I changed the example to an imaginary story about cookies that she and her younger brother would get, she understood immediately. In my story, each child received the number of cookies corresponding to their ages (twelve and eight). So she would get twelve cookies and her brother would get eight. Then I asked her how many each would have if there were 40 cookies, using the same ratio. She immediately figured out that she would get 24 cookies and her brother would get only 16! Needless to say, she loved the idea of distributing cookies based on age ratios.

Even if you don't feel as competent with math as the father in this example, realize that you can still find ways to make your child's math homework playful, fun, and relevant to her own life. You might even gain a better understanding of mathematics yourself!

In the following example, a mother reported how she used nonsense play to help her daughter with grammar homework.

Vanessa (age nine) was supposed to circle the adjective phrases in a series of sentences. The first example on her worksheet was the following sentence: *I placed the book with red covers in the middle of the pile.* In this sentence, "with red covers" is an adjective phrase. When I attempted to explain this concept to her, she became increasingly frustrated, suddenly left the dining room table where we were working, and retreated to the living room couch, pouting and sulking. The instructions on her worksheet explained that the sentences would still make sense without the adjective phrases. This information gave me the idea for a playful activity. I joined her on the couch and read different versions of the sentence by omitting various parts. I purposely included some silly phrases to make her laugh (for example: *I placed the middle of the pile*). After several nonsense versions, I read the sentence with all the words except for the adjective phrase (*I placed the book in the middle of the pile*). She immediately understood that the phrase "with red covers" was the adjective phrase, because the sentence still made sense without it. She jumped up, returned to the dining room table with a smile, and effortlessly completed her homework without any further assistance.

When your child must memorize facts or concepts, you can encourage her to use her strongest learning style. A child who learns best through images will benefit from drawing pictures or creating images in her mind to help her recall the facts. If your child has good organizational skills, you can suggest that he make lists, flash cards, or summary charts. If she learns best through social interaction, you can make a game of quizzing each other. A kinesthetic learner will learn best through hands-on activities and movement. Invite him to use building materials or act out concepts with his body. If your child is musical, help her create a song with the facts or concepts. Below are two examples of playful activities based on different learning styles.

> Julie was helping her nine-year-old daughter and a friend memorize the multiplication products for the square numbers (4, 9, 16, 25, 36, 49, etc.). To make it more fun, she asked the girls to form each of the products with their two bodies. For example, they formed the number 16 by having one girl lie down on the rug perfectly straight (to represent the digit 1) while the other lay down next to her in the opposite direction, and curved her arms around to represent the digit 6. The girls (who both loved gymnastics) had great fun doing this and soon memorized the square number products.

> Eleven-year-old Sally, a creative and musical child, was having trouble memorizing the capitals of the U.S. states until she composed a song that incorporated the names of the capitals in it.

Power-reversal games can be effective for a child who feels frustrated while struggling with a difficult homework assignment. You can have a stuffed animal (such as a teddy bear) play the role of a clueless child who misinterprets the assignment, holds the book or worksheet upside down, makes silly mistakes, keeps forgetting the right answer, and so on. Make the animal struggle, complain, and agonize about the difficult assignment. You can also play this role yourself. The goal is to encourage your child to laugh and release tensions. Your child may surprise you by finding the assignment easier after this playful activity.

Active power-reversal play can also help a child who cannot seem to concentrate well and needs to release stress. Here's an example that a mother reported to me.

When my son, Tommy, was eight years old, he was often sullen and moody while doing his homework. At those times, I would suggest the following game. While sitting on my bed, he clutched a pillow in his arms, and I had one minute to try to take it away from him. It was amazing how much strength he had. He used a lot of energy to hold onto the pillow, and he giggled a lot every time when I was about to take it away. But at the last second, he managed to get it back and hold it even tighter. He was always delighted that I faked weakness and couldn't "steal" his pillow. This game helped him vent his feelings through laughter and release a surplus of energy. He was always more relaxed afterwards, and he usually finished his homework with much better concentration and efficiency. He's eleven years old now, and sometimes we still play this game. But now I no longer need to fake weakness. He beats me easily and loves it!

Sometimes children burst into tears when they feel frustrated by a homework assignment. This would not be a good time to engage your child in a playful activity. The most helpful response is to allow the meltdown to run its course while giving your child empathy. After crying, she may surprise you by needing no further assistance or support. If she still finds the assignment too difficult, she may be ready for a playful activity or another kind of assistance.

I recommend the same guidelines for children's music education as for homework. It is not your job to *make* your children practice. When children desire to play a musical instrument, they will naturally *want* to practice the instrument because they will find pleasure in becoming increasingly proficient. Realize, however, that your child's self-initiated practice schedule might not be exactly what her music teacher recommends. Many children learn best through spurts of intense activity followed by several days or even weeks of non-activity.

You can support your child's musical education by listening to her play the instrument and accompanying her on another instrument if you have the skill to do so. Try to use the word "play" rather than "practice." If your child sees you playing an instrument for your own enjoyment, she will naturally tend to imitate you. Playing an instrument should be fun, just like other forms of play. Encourage your child to play freely *with* the instrument by making all the possible sounds with it and creating her own melodies. You can even record her compositions or write them down if you are familiar with musical notation. Remember that creativity arises out of play.

Children do not develop an urge for systematic mastery until the age of seven or eight years, so you cannot expect a younger child to conform to a regular practice schedule or even understand this concept. A spontaneous, playful approach is therefore especially important during early childhood. After seven years of age, your child may surprise you by becoming spontaneously more methodical in her practice schedule, and she may even enjoy keeping track of the amount of time she plays her instrument or the number of pieces she has mastered.

If your child never wants to play the instrument, even though you join her and make it fun, there is no point in forcing her to do so. She will not make much progress, and you will both become frustrated. Perhaps she would prefer another instrument or activity. Maybe she will want to stop taking lessons and resume them at a later time. Remember that your children have an entire lifetime to learn. The famous educator, John Holt, started learning to play the cello when he was forty years old and become proficient enough to play in string quartets. His book, *Never Too Late: My Musical Life Story*, describes his experience.

Note: See Part 3 for tips on helping your child cope with school stress and also prepare for difficult events (such as exams or performances).

Playful activities for homework

- Free play when your child comes home from school

- Make homework playful, fun, and relevant to your child's life

- Nonsense play (ex: make the assignments silly)

- Power-reversal games for frustration with difficult assignments or lack of concentration

Chapter 10

Bedtime

BEDTIME CONFLICTS can cause considerable stress for families. A major cause of bedtime problems is the fact that young children frequently have fears, which make them afraid to sleep alone. These children are not resisting sleep but rather the separation from their parents. Don't forget that your children are mammals and that the young of all land mammals sleep next to their mothers for warmth, protection, and nourishment. Children may be genetically programmed to resist separation at bedtime.

Some parents find that co-sleeping reduces bedtime struggles. The practice of co-sleeping is common in traditional cultures and is becoming more prevalent in the industrialized nations of Europe and North America. Co-sleeping can involve sharing the same bed or sleeping in separate beds but in the same room. Other parents meet their children's need for closeness by staying with them until they fall asleep even though the children sleep in a separate room.

Bedtime fears can also result from trauma. If your child's fear of sleeping alone arises after a traumatic event, you can use symbolic play to help him overcome the trauma (in addition to letting him sleep near you). Here is an example from one of my clients.

Three-year old Fiona developed a sudden fear of sleeping alone after their home was burglarized in the family's absence during the summer holidays. Until then, she had slept alone in a separate room. The parents were also traumatized,

and they recognized that their own fear may have been con-
tagious. I advised the mother to let Fiona sleep in the same
room as the parents until everybody's fear subsided. I also
recommended play with a stuffed animal family and a story
about a thief. I told the mother to let Fiona take the lead in
this make-believe story and to encourage laughter. Fiona's
fear gradually subsided.

Another source of bedtime fears is your child's own imagination.
These fears are most common between three and eight years of age.
You can address these fears with the use of symbolic play, as I did
with my daughter in the following example.

At four years of age, Sarah developed a fear of crocodiles
under the bed. This fear kept her awake even when I remained in her room with her. I helped her overcome it with
a baby crocodile puppet. I role played the baby crocodile
who felt frightened of wild animals and wanted protection. I repeated this game whenever she expressed a fear of
crocodiles. Sarah always laughed during this game and then
relaxed enough to fall asleep.

This playful activity helped my daughter release tensions, overcome
her fear, and feel connected to me at a time when she felt especially
fragile and vulnerable.

Stress from your child's day can also contribute to bedtime
problems because children who feel sad or angry about something
that happened cannot easily fall asleep. One of the most helpful
bedtime activities is simply to listen to your child. He may want to
share some upsets from the day. Perhaps another child acted mean
to him at school, or maybe something frightened him. You can have
a bedtime ritual of asking your child to share things that made him
feel angry, sad, frightened, and happy during the day.

Sometimes children need to have a good cry before they can
relax enough to sleep, and they may find a pretext to do so. For example, their favorite pajamas are in the laundry. If you calmly accept

your child's need to release pent-up stress through healing tears, he will probably cry hard but then fall asleep more quickly than if you try to distract him from crying.

Some children benefit from more active play at bedtime. However, I don't recommend energetic bedtime play unless your child is already acting that way. Be aware that intense activity can increase your child's heart rate, which could make it more difficult for him to settle down. However, if your child is *already* acting in a hyperactive or agitated way, a good power-reversal pillow fight with laughter can provide a healthy outlet for his energy and help him release stress. You can then engage him in more quiet and calming activities.

If your child refuses to get ready for bed, a few minutes of nonsense play may help. For example, let him put his pajamas on backwards, or tell him that it's time to brush his toes (instead of his teeth). Your child's laughter will provide some stress release and increase his willingness to cooperate.

Additional forms of play can help your child feel safe and connected at bedtime. Any activity with body contact, such as a back rub or a foot massage, can make your child feel connected and relaxed. Regression games can be useful for a child who has had a stressful day. Rock him in your arms like a baby, play peek-a-boo, or play with his toes.

Don't assume that lullabies are only for babies. Your older child may also enjoy bedtime songs. Every culture has its own lullabies. Sing the ones that you and your child know and love the best. If you don't know any lullabies, sing any song that you know. Invite your child to sing with you if he wishes.

Reading stories is a well-known bedtime activity. Be sure to select stories that do not contain any frightening scenes. Try switching off the light and telling a well-known story in the dark. Or make up a new, cooperative story by inviting your child to contribute to it.

If you have an ongoing bedtime struggle with your child, you may be able to resolve the issue if you discuss the problem with him (perhaps at a family meeting) and try to reach a mutually agreeable solution. Perhaps your child wants you to stay with him until he falls asleep. There is no harm in catering to this need and staying with your child even if he requests this for many years. Maybe your child wants to read in bed for a while but needs you to come back to give him a hug and turn off the light. Perhaps your child resents being told when to go to bed and wants you to trust his judgment. Children can learn to take responsibility for this decision sometime between six and twelve years of age. Whatever solution you decide on, remember to remain flexible and willing to try something new. Your child may need one bedtime routine for a few weeks but prefer another later on.

To summarize, the major keys to successful bedtime are to meet your child's needs for closeness and connection, help your child release stress through talking, crying, play, or laughter, and allow your child to develop autonomy about when to go to bed.

Playful activities for bedtime

- Symbolic play that addresses bedtime fears

- Active power-reversal games, but only if child is already agitated (ex: pillow fights)

- Nonsense play in which you let your child act silly (ex: toe brushing instead of tooth brushing)

- Activities with body contact (ex: back rubs, foot massages)

- Regression games

- Lullabies

- Story books and cooperative stories

Part 3

Using Attachment Play to Help Your Child Through Difficult Times

CHILDREN'S CHALLENGING BEHAVIOR often occurs because of stress or unhealed trauma. Therefore, an important part of non-punitive discipline is to help children cope with stress and heal from past trauma. This section addresses specific sources of stress or trauma, all of which can lead to later behavior problems if children do not heal from them. You will learn how to use various forms of play to help your children release stress and regain emotional stability.

Please realize that your children's difficulties may not be your fault. Life itself is often stressful, and children experience many hardships while growing up, even with the most loving parents. Don't forget the potential emotional impact of birth trauma or early medical interventions. Also, children with developmental disorders or a highly sensitive temperament may become more easily frustrated or overwhelmed than other children, resulting in difficult behavior. However, even though your children's difficulties may not be your fault, *you can always be part of the solution* by helping them cope with life's challenges.

Chapter 1

Birth Trauma

BIRTH IS OFTEN THE FIRST major trauma in a child's life. Although you may find it hard to believe, there is evidence that many young children between two and four years of age can remember their own birth as well as the emotions of terror or powerlessness that they felt while being born.

Birth is not inherently traumatic, but unfortunately, many births end up being difficult and traumatic for both mother and baby. Sources of potential trauma for the infant include a premature birth, an extremely long labor, a breech birth, lack of oxygen, and strangulation by the umbilical cord. Also, it's possible that medical interventions such as the use of forceps or vacuum extraction can traumatize an infant, as can rough handling and separation from the mother. A Cesarean birth may also be traumatic for the baby, especially if the surgery was an emergency.

Researchers have found that babies who had a traumatic birth often cry more than those who had easier births. In fact, babies whose births were especially traumatic may have daily crying spells for several months. This crying may be an attempt to heal from the emotional impact of the trauma.

For these birth-traumatized babies who cry a lot, a play-based approach may not be appropriate during the first few months. If your baby cries for no apparent reason (after you have checked for all immediate needs and medical conditions), she may simply need to cry. Rather than trying to distract her with a playful activity, you can hold her lovingly in your arms and offer love, comfort, and reassurance while she releases tensions through healing tears. (See my books *The Aware Baby* and *Tears and Tantrums* for more information about this crying-in-arms approach.)

Birth traumatized babies sometimes show symptoms of stress as they grow older, such as fears, frequent night waking, and aggressive or uncooperative behavior. The experience of being stuck in the birth canal during a long labor can result in a fear of tunnels or resistance to having shirts pulled down over their head. The experience of being tangled up in the umbilical cord can lead to strong refusal to be strapped into a car seat. These symptoms are more likely to appear if your baby did not heal completely by crying in arms during the first year.

You can help your birth-traumatized toddler by continuing to accept her need to cry (including tantrums!). You can also use a play-based approach when she is not crying. An effective kind of play is symbolic play with objects or themes relating to the specific kind of birth trauma that she experienced. This is called birth-simulation play. The following example from one of my clients illustrates active birth-simulation play with a child following a Cesarean birth.

> Jenny's mother had an emergency Cesarean section following ten hours of active labor, including several hours of pushing. Jenny had cried a lot during the first few months after birth. Unaware of the healing effects of crying in arms, her mother tried to stop the crying through repeated rocking and nursing for comfort. At 15 months of age, Jenny began to show signs of pent-up stress. She had difficulty falling asleep in the evening, awakened several times during the night, and sometimes hit her mother. At my suggestion, the mother engaged Jenny in two forms of play. In the first game, she covered Jenny with a few pillows and asked, "Where's Jenny?" When Jenny popped out from under the pillows, the mother faked surprise and said, "There you are!" In the second game, the mother sat on a couch with Jenny standing in front of her. The mother held Jenny prisoner between her knees while asking, "Can you get out?" She let

her struggle a little before loosening her grip. When Jenny escaped, the mother exclaimed with mock surprise, "You got away!" In both of these games, the mother encouraged laughter and repeated the game as many times as Jenny wanted. After the mother began to play these games, Jenny's sleep improved and her aggressive behavior decreased.

The self-initiated activity in the first game (popping out) helped the child heal from the feelings of powerlessness and loss of control that may have been caused by her emergency Cesarean birth. In the second game, the success at breaking free after an initial period of active struggling counteracted the feelings of frustration and fear caused by hours of unproductive labor.

The following example, reported by a mother, further illustrates active birth-simulation play following a Cesarean birth.

My son had an unplanned C-section. When he was 18 months old, I made a blanket womb tent out of his old baby gym and added a tunnel out of it by using a chair with red blankets draped over it. He loved crawling into his "cave." During the first week that he played in there, he would burst out of the side of the cave every time instead of crawling out through the tunnel. Eventually, he started crawling out through the tunnel entrance.

When children laugh during these kinds of activities, it indicates that they are releasing pent-up tensions, fears, and frustrations.

If you experienced a long, difficult labor, your child may hesitate to crawl through a tunnel as a toddler. If so, you can make the tunnel shorter or less dark. Perhaps you can move a stuffed animal through the tunnel first. It's also important for your child to be able to see you at the end of the tunnel while you encourage her to crawl through it. Remember to make the activity as silly and funny as possible.

Separation from the mother after birth can also be traumatic. During the following play coaching session, a mother re-enacted her daughter's birth symbolically with the use of dolls while telling her daughter the story of her birth, including the separation from each other.

> A mother brought her four-year-old daughter, Emily, for a parent-child play session. Emily had been separated from her mother for several hours after birth, and her mother felt that this separation had been traumatic for both of them. During the play session, the mother used a mother doll and a baby doll to tell Emily the story of her birth through play re-enactment. After the baby doll was "born," the mother put it far away from the mother doll and said, "The mother is sad because her baby has been taken away from her, and the baby is sad too." She then made the connection with their own experience, "I was so sad and angry when they took you away from me in the hospital." Emily watched this play with interest and eagerly joined in. They re-enacted the birth several more times, and changed the story so that the mother doll cuddled with the baby doll after the imaginary birth. Later, Emily wanted to act like a baby, so I encouraged her mother to wrap her in a blanket, cuddle her like a baby, and feed her water from a baby bottle. Emily gazed into her mother's eyes, beaming with pleasure.

Regression play, as described at the end of the previous example, can be helpful for children who experienced an interruption during the important bonding time after birth.

An incubator experience after birth can add additional trauma by prolonging the mother-child separation. Here is an example from one of my clients who used birth-simulation play combined with a separation game (peek-a-boo) to help her daughter recover from a traumatic incubator experience.

> At twelve months of age, Debbie awakened every night and did not go back to sleep for one to two hours. She had been born three weeks early under epidural anesthesia. A

few days after birth, she had been kept in an incubator for two days of light treatment. When her mother consulted with me, I recommended the crying-in-arms approach at bedtime and also during the night to help Debbie work through these traumas. I also recommended daytime birth-simulation play with a large cardboard box (a symbolic incubator). The mother encouraged Debbie to crawl into and out of the big box, and the two of them played peek-a-boo and other laughter games while she was in the box. After the mother implemented these ideas, Debbie began to sleep better.

Playful activities for children who experienced a traumatic birth

- Symbolic play with props or themes relating to the specific birth trauma (birth-simulation play)

- Regression games

- Separation games if the baby experienced separation from the mother

---

Chapter 2

Birth of a Sibling

THE BIRTH OF A SIBLING can be one of the most stressful events in the life of a child. No matter how well you have prepared your child for a new brother or sister, the reality of a baby in the home can be stressful or even traumatic for him. He may express this stress through aggressive or obnoxious behavior, stubbornness, regression, or unwillingness to cooperate. Luckily, several forms of play can help your child continue to feel loved, allow him to release emotions, and accept the presence of a new sibling.

It's important to reassure your older child that he has not lost your love. An effective way to communicate your love and maintain your connection with him is to arrange times for nondirective child-centered play. You will need to do this when the baby is sleeping or when someone else is available to be with the baby. Researchers have found that as little as half an hour once a week of this kind of play can be effective in transforming children's challenging behaviors. Daily play sessions would be even better.

In addition to nondirective play, you can also engage your child in symbolic play with dolls or stuffed animals that represent your family. This is the activity that I recommend most frequently for children with a new sibling. Here is an example of a play session that I conducted with a four-year-old boy while his parents watched.

Four-year-old Andy showed jealousy and behavior problems after the birth of his sister. I presented him with a bear family consisting of four stuffed bears: two large ones, a smaller one, and a baby bear. I acted the part of the baby by pretending to cry, and he pretended to change the baby bear's diaper. He laughed heartily while announcing that the baby bear kept wetting her diaper. For some reason, he found that hilarious. He then became involved in acting out a long story in which the boy bear went on an airplane trip with the parents while the baby bear stayed home.

This child began by finding a way to laugh, and then he expressed emotions and wishes by creating a story about a boy taking a trip with his parents but without his baby sister. Laughter that occurs during this kind of play helps children release feelings of anger and jealousy, and symbolic story elements help children further process their emotions.

If your child doesn't enjoy playing with stuffed animals or dolls, you can create a symbolic family with other kinds of toys.

A mother consulted with me about her three-year-old son who was jealous after the birth of his baby brother. When I suggested the bear family game, she replied that her son didn't like to play with stuffed animals. I asked her what he liked to play with, and she replied that he preferred trains. So I suggested that she play a train family game with him, using train engines to represent the members of their family. She later reported that her son willingly engaged in the play and laughed heartily.

I recommend playing these games at least once a day with your child, if possible, following the birth of a sibling. Parents generally report improved behavior in their children after several play episodes of this nature.

Power-reversal games can also help, especially if your older child acts aggressively. Many children take their anger out on the baby. The following example from one of my clients illustrates power-reversal play after the birth of a sibling.

A mother consulted with me about her two-year-old son who had started acting aggressively after the birth of his brother six months previously. This difficult behavior had recently increased, and she was at a loss to know how to change it. During the consultation, I made several suggestions, including power-reversal play at times when their son acted aggressively toward the baby. The mother later sent a follow-up note thanking me for the consultation. She reported that their son greatly enjoyed pushing mom and dad instead of his baby brother. Everyone had laughed during the play, and the entire mood of their family had improved. She thanked me for the new tools in their parenting toolbox, and said that they planned to continue these playful activities.

If you don't have the energy to engage your child in active power-reversal play, you can do a symbolic version of it, as the following example describes (reported by a mother).

During my pregnancy, and after my daughter was born, I was very fragile and found it hard to do the necessary rough-and-tumble play with my five-year-old son when he was angry or frustrated. We discovered that it sometimes worked well for me to make a pillow talk with a squeaky voice, saying things like "no, don't hit me, don't stamp on me." On one occasion after the birth, he announced that one of the pillows was a baby pillow. So I said in a squeaky voice, "Don't hit the baby pillow! Stop it! Stop it!" He loved this play and laughed heartily while attacking the pillow.

To represent the baby, you can also use drawings or clay models. When you encourage your child to hit an object that symbolizes the new baby, you will *not* increase his aggressive behavior toward his sibling. On the contrary, this kind of play will help him feel understood, allow him to release anger and anxiety, and make him *less* aggressive in real life.

Some children direct their aggression at the parents. From a young child's point of view, you, the parent, are to blame for bringing a new baby into your home, and it is only natural that your child will feel some anger toward you. But your child may also feel afraid of losing your love if he shows too much anger. These conflicting feelings can cause considerable stress for him.

If your child yells at you or hits you, try to avoid an angry response. If you yell back at him or use isolation as punishment (timeout), you will only reinforce his feeling that his connection with you is fragile. Instead, you can engage him in a playful pillow fight, as described in the example above. During this kind of play, your child will release anger through laughter and learn that his anger will not destroy the bond between you.

Regression play is also useful after the birth of a sibling. Some children spontaneously start acting like a baby after their sibling's birth, and these children will probably benefit from regression games. If you treat your child like a baby, you will help him feel nurtured and loved at a time when he might be feeling confused, anxious, or unloved. In the following example, I recommended both regression play and power-reversal play.

When seven-year-old Caroline's sister was three months old, her father consulted with me because of his concern about Caroline's behavior. He described her as emotionally shut down, because she had difficulty expressing herself. He also reported that she frequently acted like a baby. The father had remarried, and the baby's mother was not Caroline's mother, so Caroline may have been additionally stressed by missing her own mother. I advised the father to avoid telling her to act like a big girl and to encourage the baby theme instead. I suggested that he could playfully wrap her in a blanket, cuddle and rock her, sing to her, and feed her. I also suggested power-reversal games in which he could invite her to knock him down with pillows. I explained that Caroline needed to express anger in a safe way, and that laughter was an important form of emotional release.

Another helpful kind of play is a form of nonsense play in which both parents pretend to argue with each other about whose turn it is to play with the older child. This game works best with children over four years of age. Most children love this game and laugh heartily while their parents pretend to fight for the privilege of being with them. It's helpful to end this game with an activity in which *both* parents play with the child in a cooperative way. For example, you can each hold two corners of a blanket to create a hammock and rock your child back and forth while singing. It may be difficult for both parents to be available at the same time when there is a new baby in the family, but if you can manage to do this activity with your older child once in a while, it will probably be worth your efforts.

Note: See Part 2, Chapter 7 for tips on how to deal playfully with sibling rivalry if it continues after the baby's newborn period.

Playful activities for children after the birth of a sibling

- Nondirective child-centered play

- Symbolic play with a teddy bear family

- Power-reversal games

- Regression games

- Nonsense play (ex: parents pretend to "fight" for the privilege of playing with the child)

Chapter 3

Parental Divorce

WHEN PARENTS GET DIVORCED, the children experience a variety of painful emotions, including sadness, anxiety, anger, guilt, confusion, powerlessness, embarrassment, and loyalty conflicts. These emotions can be at the root of behavior problems, such as aggression, unwillingness to cooperate, reluctance to attend school, or difficulty concentrating in school.

Children of divorce need stability, reassurance, connection, and lots of love. Most of the play-based activities described in Part 1 are beneficial for children of divorce, specifically symbolic play (with the theme of divorce), contingency play, nonsense play, separation games, power-reversal games, regression games, all activities with body contact, and cooperative games.

If your child is still young enough to enjoy playing with stuffed animals, dolls, or puppets, you can introduce symbolic play with an animal family just like your own. Act out the story of your family by explaining, for example: "The mommy bear and the daddy bear didn't get along very well anymore, so they decided to live in different places. The daddy went to live in this house over here, and the mommy went to live in another house over here. But they both loved the baby bear and wanted to live with her. So they agreed that the baby bear would live with the mommy part of the time and with the daddy part of the time. Even though the mommy and the daddy didn't want to live with each other anymore, they both loved their baby and would continue to love her forever."

If your child becomes involved in this play, you can begin to explore emotions together. You can say, for example: "How do you think the baby bear felt when the daddy bear moved to another house? Was she mad at her daddy for leaving?" If your child agrees that the baby bear felt mad, you can invite her to make the baby bear kick the daddy bear. You can act this out or invite your child to do it with the animals. If this symbolic play causes your child to laugh, you are on the right track. If your child takes the lead and develops the story further, let her do so. By playing in this symbolic way with your child, you are letting her know that you understand and accept her emotions. At the same time, you are telling a story that provides her with accurate information and reassurance that you will never abandon her.

Sometimes children invent their own therapeutic games with symbolic elements. Here is an example that a divorced mother reported to me.

When Danielle was three years old, her father decided to leave our family in pursuit of another relationship. He had chosen to move to an apartment at an undisclosed location. He would periodically come into our family home to say hello to Danielle, pick up clothes and other items, and head back to his apartment. When my daughter asked him if she could go with him, he always said "no." When she asked him where his apartment was, he refused to tell her. This caused great strife, confusion, and hurt feelings for her and also for me. After a couple of weeks of this pattern, there was an incident where my daughter wanted to go with him, and he said "no" (as usual). He closed the front door and left her crying and raging on the stairs inside our home. I supported her in this emotional release until she had finished crying. The next day, as we left the house to go shopping, she stopped at the front door and told me to go out, so I did. Then she slammed the door while remaining inside. I slowly opened the door and she laughed hysterically. Then she directed me to go outside and she slammed the door again. I peeked in and saw that she was laughing hysterically again. She then asked me to come inside and sit on the stairs next to her. She buried her head on the stairs and pretended to cry, peeking up at me periodically and laughing. Then she stood up, walked out the front door, and slammed it. When she opened it, I pretended to cry and beat my hands on the stairs, and she started laughing. We played this game for about an hour. After that day, Danielle didn't have a problem with her father leaving. She also handled my permanent separation from her father and subsequent move to another state with ease. In the years to follow, she periodically reminded me of that day when we had played together at the front door, and we always had a good laugh.

In this example, the child spontaneously invented a therapeutic game, which included a symbolic aspect of the father's departure from the family (slamming the front door). The mother participated in the play in a helpful way by encouraging the game to continue and by engaging in role reversal while letting her daughter take the lead.

The above example included an element of separation (one person inside the house and one outside the house). Other separation games, such as hide-and-seek, will help your child deal with fear of abandonment, so be sure to play these kinds of games as much as possible.

Contingency play can help your child regain a sense of control at a time when she feels powerless to change the course of events. For example, give her piggy-back rides in which you let her indicate which way to turn. This game also provides a great way to connect physically with your child.

To help your child release anger (possibly directed at you), engage her in frequent power-reversal games in which you invite her to knock you over with a pillow, bury you under pillows, lock you up in an imaginary cage, or attack you with a plastic spider. Play your part by pretending to be scared and weak. If your child feels angry at the absent parent, you can ask her to draw a picture of him or create a clay model of him. Then invite her to scribble on the picture or pound the clay model with her fist. As she destroys the drawing or clay model, pretend to be the absent parent under attack and make dramatic sounds of agony. The more your child laughs, the more she will release her anger. If you are harboring anger at your ex-partner, this exercise may also be therapeutic for you!

Nonsense play can add a humorous element to a topic that would otherwise feel serious and distressing. The following example of one of my clients describes the use of power-reversal play and nonsense play for helping a child through parental divorce.

> Five-year-old Billy became uncooperative, aggressive, and disruptive after his parents separated, and after he moved with his mother and younger brother to live with an aunt in another part of the city. He frequently tried to hit his brother, mother, and aunt. I explained to the mother that Billy blamed her for leaving his father and that his anger needed a healthy release. I advised her to encourage laughter through two kinds of power-reversal play: hitting the mother with a pillow while she fakes weakness and falls down, and locking up his mother in an imaginary cage made of chairs. These games helped Billy release his aggression through laughter and play. A year and a half later, after the divorce was finalized, the mother became engaged to another man, and Billy's aggressive behavior returned. She consulted with me again, and I advised both the mother and her fiancé to engage Billy in power-reversal play. I also suggested a form on nonsense play in which she and Billy would pronounce the word "divorce" in silly ways and laugh about it together.

Some parents think that they must stop aggressive behavior rather than encourage it. However, allowing your child to hit you in a playful pillow fight or destroy a picture of her father (or mother) will not cause her to become more aggressive. On the contrary, it will help her release anger through laughter and decrease her desire for violence or revenge.

Cooperative games can be a great antidote for children of divorce. When the home atmosphere has been full of strife and antagonism between the parents, a cooperative game can feel reassuring to your children and offer a pleasant diversion. By playing games cooperatively instead of competitively, your children will regain trust in your ability to be on their side and work together toward a common goal.

If your child wants to act like a baby, don't be afraid to treat her like a precious, helpless infant. This regression play on her part may be her way of bringing back memories from a time when your family was happier. If you let her act like a baby for a while, she will soak up your attention, and this will strengthen her to cope with your new family situation.

By playing with your children in these various ways, you can help them navigate through the trauma that divorce has caused in your family. In addition to the play-based activities discussed in this chapter, children of divorce can benefit from group or individual therapy. The advantage of group therapy is that the children can form a common bond with other children of divorce. This connection can reduce their feelings of alienation or of being different from other children. These other sources of support and healing will be especially beneficial immediately before and after the divorce when everybody's emotions are at their peak, and when you (understandably) might not have the time or emotional resources necessary for play-based interactions with your children.

Playful activities to help children
cope with their parents' divorce

- Symbolic play with props or themes relating to divorce (ex: a teddy bear family game in which the parents get divorced)

- Separation games (ex: hide-and-seek)

- Contingency play (ex: piggy-back rides).

- Power-reversal games (ex: let your child knock you down with a pillow or destroy a drawing or clay model of the absent parent)

- Nonsense play (ex: pronounce the word "divorce" in silly ways)

- Cooperative games and activities

- Regression games

Chapter 4

Natural Disasters and Terrorism

WE CANNOT KNOW when a fire, flood, earthquake, hurricane, tornado, or terrorist attack will occur. Because of the unpredictable nature of these terrifying events, it is impossible to prepare children for them. A big part of the trauma results from this sudden, unexpected aspect, which can make children (and adults) feel powerless and vulnerable. A natural reaction for children (and also for adults) is to think that it could happen again and to be on the alert for this possibility. A physiological state of hyper-arousal usually accompanies this mental alertness.

The major behavioral difficulties following these unexpected traumas include clinginess, refusal to go to bed or to school, difficulty sleeping, and regression to earlier stages of development.

Even if you cannot prepare your children for such events, you can play an important role by helping your children heal from the trauma after it has occurred. Don't forget that crying and raging are important healing mechanisms. After the terrorist attacks on September 11th in New York City, parents of young children who had witnessed the tragedy reported that their children's temper tantrums increased during several months afterwards. These tantrums probably represented the children's need to release tensions in order to heal from the impact of the trauma.

Sometimes children begin screaming about some minor event that triggers a trauma memory. For example, a child who has survived a major fire might start crying when somebody lights a match. But some events that trigger tantrums appear to have no relationship to the original trauma. A child who has survived a hurricane might throw a tantrum because you serve him the wrong kind of cereal for breakfast (the "broken-cookie phenomenon"). When a child feels an overload of stress and needs to cry, almost anything will serve as a pretext to trigger a meltdown. In all of these situations, it's important to remain loving and supportive while allowing the tantrum to run its course. See my book *Tears and Tantrums* for more information about crying.

Play can also be very useful for helping children heal from traumatic events. Children spontaneously incorporate elements of trauma in their play. A mother described the following incident to me.

> A wildfire recently destroyed over 300 homes in our city. We didn't have to evacuate, but my parents, who live in the same city, had to evacuate to our home as the fire approached their home. For several days, they did not know if their home had survived the fire. During that period, I noticed one day that my daughter (age five) pretended that one of her dolls was afraid of a fire, and she created an imaginary scene that helped the doll feel safe.

If your child has been frightened by a natural disaster, begin with a nondirective approach in which you observe and support your child's choice of play activities. Children who feel safe enough in the play context will usually spontaneously bring up the trauma theme in their play and find a way to heal with your loving attention.

If you think your child can handle a more direct approach, you can suggest symbolic play with specific props or themes that involve elements of the event. For example, if there has been a fire in your neighborhood, you can offer your child a toy fire truck and suggest a play theme about a fire. This approach is most effective when you create a safe, playful context and encourage emotional release in the form of laughter. Through play, your child can gradually heal from the trauma.

A playful approach with laughter is often sufficient to help children work through most traumas caused by natural disasters. Here is an example of the use of play therapy with my own daughter following an earthquake.

When Sarah was twelve years old, we experienced an early-morning earthquake. I ran into her room to reassure her, and she clung to me, trembling and crying. However, I feared the possibility of aftershocks and couldn't give her my full attention. After that event, she felt too terrified to sleep alone in her room, so I let her sleep with me. After a few weeks with no improvement, I started sleeping on a mattress in her room, with the goal of helping her adapt to her own bed. I also started to play an earthquake game with her at bedtime. I explained the game to her and obtained her permission to play it. To begin the game, I sat on her bed in the dark for a few minutes of silence, then I suddenly yelled, "Earthquake!" while shaking her bed violently. Sarah immediately started to laugh. We played this game every evening while I continued to sleep in her room. Then one evening, after our usual earthquake game with much laughter, she said, "I'm scared," and started to cry. She continued to cry hard for several minutes while I stayed with her. Finally, she lay down in her bed and fell asleep. The following evening, she said to me, "You can sleep in your own room tonight. I'm not scared anymore." It had been exactly four weeks since the earthquake.

In this example, my daughter cried during the initial trauma but not sufficiently to prevent post-traumatic fears from developing. The playful re-enactment of the earthquake helped her release fear through therapeutic laughter, and it "paved the way" for deeper emotions to come to the surface. She cried again after we had done several play sessions, and this emotional release appeared to be the final element needed to complete her healing process.

Contingency play can counteract feelings of powerlessness and helplessness following a traumatic event. For example, give your child a piggy-back ride and let him direct you by tapping on your right or left shoulder. Depending on the age of your child, you can create a whole set of complex rules. By giving orders that you obey, your child will regain a sense of control over his world. These piggyback rides provide additional reassurance to traumatized children because they involve body contact. Following frightening experiences, children benefit from the reassurance provided by physical contact with the people who love them. Look for additional playful activities that involve touching, and be sure to hold and cuddle your child as much as he wants.

Following a natural disaster, terrorism, or war, I recommend professional therapy for your child if he has been physically injured, if a family member has been injured or killed, if he is unable to function normally (for example, refuses to eat, sleep, separate from you, or go to school), or if any post-traumatic symptom lasts more than a month. The suggestions in this chapter may help, but they may not be sufficient. Furthermore, if you yourself have also been traumatized, you may not have the necessary emotional resources to assist your child.

Playful activities to help children heal from natural disasters and terrorism

- Nondirective child-centered play

- Symbolic play with props or themes relating to the traumatic event (ex: fire truck, earthquake game)

- Contingency play (ex: piggy-back rides with the child giving commands)

- Activities with body contact

Chapter 5

Illnesses, Accidents, and Hospitalization

THIS SECTION PROVIDES tips for children who are ill or have experienced an illness, accident, or hospitalization. Accidents are frequent during childhood. Many children experience bumps, bruises, cuts, skinned knees, and sometimes even broken bones. A child's natural response to these accidents is to cry, and this crying is an important part of the healing process. All injuries lead to emotional trauma in addition to the physical trauma. Painful emotions can include confusion, fear, disappointment, or anger. That's why children's crying sometimes lasts much longer than the physical pain itself.

The most helpful approach is to pay loving attention to your child after an injury and allow the crying to run its course. After crying, children can sometimes benefit from further therapeutic interventions in the form of play and laughter. These playful activities can also help children who do not feel safe enough to cry or for whom crying is physically difficult or painful.

Symbolic play with props or themes relating to the accident can be beneficial. When children are reminded of the accident while feeling safe, they will usually laugh, and this laughter helps release the fear and anger caused by the accident.

You can use this kind of play with children, beginning in infancy. A mother reported the following example to me.

When my daughter was about five months old, she learned to roll over repeatedly without stopping. The first time she did this, she rolled right off a king-size family bed at the end of a daytime nap. Luckily, the mattress is on the floor for the children's sake, so she didn't have far to fall. But I ran to the room when I heard her screaming. She calmed down quickly after I picked her up, but she began to cry again a few minutes later when we approached the edge of the bed. Once she was done crying, I said to her, "You fell off the bed and got a big fright. Shall we talk about it?" I laid her on her stomach on the bed and then said, "You rolled, and you went boom!" As I said, "Boom," I gently rolled her onto her back and made a very surprised face as if I had just fallen on the floor. I also imitated the sound of a baby crying. She stared at me and then burst out laughing. I repeated this several times, and she laughed each time. After five or six times, the laughter dwindled to a chuckle, and after two more times, she lost interest in the game. It was a wonderful experience for me to find that, even with such a young baby, we can "talk" about the problem and heal from it through play and laughter (as well as crying). Afterwards, she was never afraid of the bed or of rolling.

A child's illness or hospitalization is a huge source of stress for the entire family. Although you may feel anxious and overwhelmed, it's important to remember that play can provide an important antidote to the seriousness of the situation. Play cannot replace the need for medical advice and treatment, but certain play-based interventions can help your child cope with the emotions caused by pain, illness, and hospitalization. Play and laughter may even help your child recover more quickly.

A useful play intervention for children who have been hospitalized is symbolic play with props or themes about doctors, hospitals, and medical interventions. Give your child a doctor kit and invite her to play freely with it. Children who have been hospitalized usually play eagerly with these materials. Join in the play if your child wishes, perhaps by playing the role of a patient. You can turn the play into a power-reversal game by pretending to be frightened or upset. If your child laughs, you are on the right track. Don't be surprised if your child wants to play doctor for weeks or even months after having been hospitalized.

The actual source of your child's trauma may differ from your assumptions. You may think that she felt most traumatized by the pain or physical discomfort, but she may have been most traumatized by the separation from you, from forced immobility, or from something else (for example, an inability to see if her eyes were bandaged). Maybe the hardest part of her experience was lack of knowledge about what would happen. Her play with a doctor kit and hospital theme will probably reveal what she found most difficult.

Even minor accidents or medical procedures can be stressful for children and can leave them feeling frightened and vulnerable. A mother reported the following experience.

I brought my daughter (age seven) to the hospital emergency room one evening because of stomach pains. It turned out to be nothing serious, and they eventually sent us home. But she has had lots of fears since then and is terrified that she might have to go there again. She has been crying a lot and telling me all her fears, and I've been listening to her feelings. I also suggested that we could play doctor, but at first she didn't want to play. A few days ago, she finally agreed to play doctor, and she laughed a lot. I pretended that I had a crocodile in my stomach, and I complained loudly about how much my stomach hurt with that creature inside. She laughed and told me that she would keep me in the hospital a long time and make me come back again. Then she brought her doll and told me that the doll was a nurse who accidentally dropped her eyeballs in my stomach, and that now I needed to stay in the hospital to get the eyeballs out! We both laughed a lot. I could see that she felt much better after this play.

If your child is chronically ill, your entire family will probably feel stressed. If your child has enough energy to sit up and play with toys, she will probably benefit from nondirective play sessions in which you let her direct the play while you follow her lead. These sessions will strengthen your relationship with her and also help her work through disturbing emotions. With the use of small toys, you can conduct these play sessions while your child sits in bed. In all of these play activities, be sure to encourage laughter. Remember that laughter can reduce anxiety, strengthen the immune system, and decrease physical pain.

Older children, too, can benefit from various forms of play during illness. In the following example, a mother described how she helped her son cope with a frightening medical diagnosis. She used several play-based approaches, including symbolic play and power-reversal play.

When Sam was eight years old, he was diagnosed with a hole in the upper chamber of his heart (atrial septal defect). One of the symptoms was that he would get tired quickly when exercising or playing outside. It also meant that he would have a shortened life expectancy (about 15 years less than average). During the next three years, we consulted several pediatric cardiologists for medical examinations and advice, some of which was contradictory. Luckily, the hole eventually closed up on its own, so Sam did not need surgery. During that three-year period we used therapeutic play, which greatly helped him process his thoughts and feelings about what he was going through. The initial diagnosis was frightening and shocking, and subsequent doctor visits were like an emotional roller coaster ride. Shortly after the initial diagnosis, I asked him to draw what it felt like to have a hole in his heart. His drawings were angry scribbles at first. Then they evolved to drawings of people with holes in their hearts. I also had him take a pillow and do what he wanted to it to show what he was feeling. These play therapy sessions often ended up in pillow fights with me playfully overreacting when he hit me. His initial anger turned into laughter, and sometimes he cried. I also used clay, asking him to shape it according to how he was feeling. He would usually make sculptures of people or animals with holes in their hearts. Sometimes, he would give them to me as a gift. Other times, he would keep them in a special place in his room and occasionally bring them to me, seemingly out of the blue. I learned that the best time to talk about his medical condition was when he would bring these clay figures to me.

If your child must go through difficult medical procedures, you can use play during the procedures to make them more fun and to increase your child's willingness to cooperate. Instead of focusing your child's attention on pain or fear, this kind of play brings your child's attention *away* from the distress. The laughter that occurs will help her relax and cooperate. An additional advantage is that your child's later memories of the procedures will be pleasant.

In the following example, a mother reported her use of play and laughter to help her daughter through some difficult medical interventions.

Sally had a feeding tube and pump until she was three years old. During those three years, she had lots of problems with vomiting (sometimes five times a day) and difficulty gaining weight. We did lots of things to play and make our situation as fun as possible during those years. During the many hours of tube feedings, we read books to her, or I would do little skits, and she would laugh and clap. I also did puppet shows, played music, and even put on little cheerleading performances for her while she was tethered to her feeding pump. We tried to make the trips to the doctors and hospital as fun as possible. I remember running through the hospital halls with Sally in the stroller while we pretended that the route was an amusement park ride. Sally is now a happy and confident five-year-old child.

If your child is very weak or ill, you can use guided fantasy play to strengthen her emotionally and bring her attention away from the illness. As in the example above, the goal is to take the child's attention *away* from the fear or pain, and to provide her with strengthening, enjoyable, and pain-free images. This approach involves creating stories that allow your child to feel powerful and strong. The most effective stories are those that feature your child as the hero and that incorporate elements of her life. Stories filled with humor, adventure, surprises, and magic are especially effective. Later on, after your child has regained her health and strength, you can use symbolic play with themes of doctors and hospitals to help her heal emotionally from the experience.

Guided fantasy play is especially effective with children who have a vivid imagination. I used this approach with my daughter, as the following example describes.

> When Sarah was between the ages of eight and twelve years, I used guided fantasy play when she had a fever or headache. I sat at her bedside with a wet washcloth and told her a story about a magic pond in a forest with a path leading to it. Lily pads covered the surface of the pond, and frogs sat on the lily pads, guarding the pond. In my story, I described how I walked down the path and dipped the washcloth into the magic water, which had special healing properties. I told the frogs that Sarah was not feeling well, and the frogs sent get-well wishes to her. Then I placed the wet washcloth on her forehead. She always felt better and stronger after this story. We called it "the magic pond."

When your child's strength returns after an illness or surgery, don't be surprised if she begins to have crying spells or even temper tantrums. These manifestations of strong emotions indicate that she is healing emotionally from the medical trauma. Children who are very ill don't have the energy to cry, so crying is actually a good sign that your child's strength and health are returning (assuming, of course, that your child is not crying because of physical pain).

Stay with your child during these outbursts, without trying to stop her. After the crying and tantrums have run their course, your child will probably feel calm, relaxed, and happy. As explained elsewhere in this book, children often use minor pretexts as emotional triggers for their tantrums (the "broken-cookie phenomenon").

Some children who have been through medical trauma (or any major trauma) regress to earlier stages of development. If your child begins to act like a baby, perhaps she wants to re-experience the comfort and warm connection she felt with you during infancy. It's fine to treat her like a baby by cuddling and rocking her, singing to her, playing baby games, and so forth.

Note: See Chapter 9 in this section for suggestions of ways to prepare children for medical interventions.

Playful activities for children following illnesses, accidents, or hospitalization

- Symbolic play (ex: role play an accident, give child a doctor kit or some clay)

- Nondirective child-centered play

- Power-reversal games

- Nonsense play with laughter to help children through medical procedures

- Guided fantasy play for an ill child: empowering stories with humor, adventure, surprises, and magic

- Regression games

Chapter 6

Separation Trauma

MOST YOUNG CHILDREN go through a period of normal separation anxiety, which begins around eight months of age and continues for a few years. During this stage, infants and toddlers will often cling to their parents (or other familiar caretakers), cry during separations, and greet their parents warmly when they return. Children this age can get used to new caretakers, but they may need several visits with a new person before they feel safe.

You can help children cope with separations by playing the game of peek-a-boo, as the following example illustrates.

When my son was between twelve and 24 months old, I sometimes left him at home with a babysitter while I went to the doctor or dentist. Although he knew the babysitter well and enjoyed being with her, he found my departure difficult and would often cry. I discovered that playing peek-a-boo with him before I left helped him cope better with the separation. I would go outside and wave to him through the open window. Then I would crouch down so he couldn't see me and suddenly jump up again, much to his delight. He always laughed heartily. After playing this game for a few minutes, I always entered the house again to give him a definite good-bye hug before departing. He never cried after these games of peek-a-boo, but cheerfully waved good-bye to me.

Prolonged separation from the parents (or other primary caregivers) during these early years can cause considerable distress for infants and young children. The longer the separation, the more traumatized the child will be. When children of any age experience permanent separations from the parents (because of departure or death), the children will be severely traumatized and may need therapeutic interventions to overcome the feelings of loss, confusion, terror, and rage.

Separation trauma can occur even in the absence of a physical separation. If you are extremely stressed, depressed, anxious, angry, or simply preoccupied, you will probably have very little time or attention for your child. Maybe you suffered from post-partum depression and were unable to form a joyful, healthy attachment to your child during the first year. Whatever the reason for the emotional distance between you and your child, it's important to understand that your child will feel abandoned whenever the relationship between you is strained.

Children who have experienced any kind of separation trauma (either through physical separation or emotional distance) often have challenging behaviors, such as aggression, clinginess, or refusal to cooperate. They can also become obnoxious and demanding.

When children have experienced separation trauma, it is especially important to avoid any form of punishment that enforces a separation between the child and the parent (the use of time-out), because nothing is more terrifying for such a child than separation. I recommend a non-punitive approach to discipline for *all* children, whether they have been traumatized or not.

Play can be very useful for helping children heal from separation trauma, whether it results from a physical separation or an emotional one. Just as with normal separation anxiety, effective therapeutic games for such children are separation games such peek-a-boo and hide-and-seek, as the following example illustrates.

Three-year-old Ellen experienced separation trauma when her mother had to be hospitalized for appendicitis. After her mother returned home, Ellen awakened frequently in the night screaming "mommy, mommy!" When her mother consulted with me, I advised her to accept Ellen's crying without trying to stop it. I also suggested that she play hide-and-seek with Ellen during the day while encouraging lots of laughter. After implementing these suggestions, Ellen's anxiety and nightmares decreased.

Body contact is also important for children who have experienced separation trauma. Close physical contact with you can help them regain a sense of safety, trust, and connection. Children are quite skilled at inventing ways to get close, but some of your children's efforts may feel inconvenient or even obnoxious to you. If you can recognize these behaviors as efforts to reconnect with you after a physical or emotional separation, perhaps you can turn them into a game.

For example, if your three-year-old son stands on your feet and wraps his arms around your knees, you could pretend that you haven't noticed him, try to walk with him on your feet, and complain bitterly about how hard it is to walk. He will probably start giggling. Alternatively, you could pretend that you are glued together. If your five-year-old daughter repeatedly and obnoxiously licks your face, you could lick her face and say: "Yum! You taste like a chocolate ice cream cone!" These playful approaches will address your child's underlying need for closeness and reassurance.

Children who have suffered from a traumatic separation may resist human contact in order to protect themselves from becoming too attached (and hurt) again. If your child resists physical closeness, it's important to respect his boundaries but to look for ways to incorporate touch into playful activities. Even the most wary children find it difficult to resist a hand-stacking game or an invitation for arm wrestling (which you can then turn into a power-reversal game). Perhaps your child will let you take his pulse or put lotion on his skin in the context of doctor play. Or you could suggest a game in which you hide toys in your sleeve or under your shirt and invite your child to find them. Maybe your child will let you catch him with a quick hug after a chasing game or hold his ankles while he walks on his hands. As your child heals from the past trauma and regains a sense of trust, he will gradually welcome more physical contact with you.

All adopted children have experienced separation from their birth mother. Those who had foster parents or lived in an orphanage before their adoption suffered additional separation traumas. The following example from one of my clients illustrates the benefits of separation games with an adopted child.

David, a little boy from Romania, had been placed in an orphanage at two days of age after his mother's death. American parents adopted him at ten months of age, and he began to show behavior problems early on. When he was three years old, a behavioral therapist recommended the use of time-out, but David's behavior only worsened. When he was four years old, the parents discovered my work, stopped using time-out, and consulted with me. They described him as strong-willed, impulsive, easily over-excited, distractible, non-compliant, aggressive, and prone to jealousy. At school he frequently hit other children, always wanted to be first, and laughed when other children got hurt. He frequently ran away and hid, both at school and at home, especially when his parents asked him to do something. A psychologist had labeled him at risk for hyperactivity, attention problems, and externalizing behaviors (such as aggression). I gave the mother tips on non-punitive discipline and recommended full acceptance of their son's crying and raging. David's frequent running away indicated to me that he was struggling with unhealed separation trauma, so I told her to play hide-and-seek and chasing games with him every day. I explained that the more he laughed, the sooner he would heal, and the quicker his behavior would improve. Eight weeks later, we had a follow-up consultation, and the mother reported dramatic improvement in her son's behavior. He acted much less aggressively at school and at home, had stopped running away, and had become more cooperative. He had much better concentration and focus during play and had begun to try some of the quieter activities at school, such as painting. In fact, he had painted a picture of a flower with great care and thoughtfulness, something that he had never done before.

This child had suffered from two major separation traumas, first from his biological mother, then from the orphanage. In addition to the game of hide-and-seek, the parents' switch to non-punitive discipline and their acceptance of his crying and raging probably also played an important role in his healing process.

Symbolic play with dolls or stuffed animals can be an effective way to tell a young child about his adoption while allowing him to work through the separation trauma. The following example from another one of my clients illustrates this use of symbolic play.

Two-year-old Trevor had been adopted at seven months of age from a Chinese orphanage. Among other play-based activities (including separation games), I suggested using a teddy bear family to tell him the story of his adoption. In a follow-up consultation, the mother reported that he loved the teddy bear activity. During the play, he started remembering events from the orphanage and talking about them! She was convinced that he remembered being in the orphanage and that the opportunity to talk about it and play it out with the teddy bears helped him make sense of the experience and work through his emotions.

I also frequently recommend regression play with adopted children who may have missed out on love and attention during their stay in an orphanage. Let your child pretend to be a baby while you cuddle and rock him in your arms.

Playful activities for children who have experienced separation trauma

• Separation games (ex: peek-a-boo, hide-and-seek, chasing games)

• Activities with body contact

• Symbolic play with a teddy bear family to act out the story of what happened

• Regression games

Chapter 7

School Stress

SCHOOL CAN BE A huge source of stress for children. Children can experience stress simply by being forced to sit for long periods of time and engage in activities that they have not freely chosen. Inappropriate teaching methods can add to children's stress and anxiety. If you or the teacher places great importance on passing tests, your child may develop test anxiety. Children with a highly sensitive temperament can become easily over-stimulated by high noise levels or bright lights. Having to complete work quickly can also overwhelm them.

Sometimes the source of stress is more serious. Needless to say, harsh discipline, a playground bully, or sexual abuse by a teacher can be terrifying for children. There is *always* a valid reason for children's fears and reluctance to go to school, and it's important to talk to the school staff about your concerns.

Children who experience school stress may not talk openly about the problem. Instead, they may fight with their siblings, have trouble sleeping, complain of headaches, resist school and homework, or withdraw from family activities and distract themselves with computer games. They may also begin to have more temper tantrums.

If you think that school stress is contributing to these behaviors, try to determine the exact source of your child's stress. Don't hesitate to contact your child's teacher or the school principal in order to resolve the issue that is troubling your child.

It's important to realize, too, that these difficult behaviors may have nothing to do with the school. Factors such as a parent's illness, depression, or alcoholism can also cause a child to feel stressed, so be sure to explore all sources of stress in your family before assuming that the school is at fault.

You can help your child cope with school stress through play. The following sections describe play-based approaches for helping children cope with three specific kinds of school-based stress: anxiety about school rules, bullying, and "mean" teachers.

Anxiety about school rules

Sometimes children develop anxiety about breaking one of the school rules even when the teacher does not use harsh discipline. This situation is more likely to occur in children who have never been punished at home. The idea of any kind of punishment (such as missing recess) can terrify such children.

In these kinds of situations, you can address the issue through play. An effective approach is to elicit laughter with exaggeration and silliness (nonsense play), as the following example with my son illustrates.

Until ten years of age, Nicky attended a school in which the teacher did not use punishment. At age ten he switched to a school with a more traditional approach to discipline. After the first day, he arrived home with a folder containing a list of school rules and consequences, which he was supposed to read with a parent. After we read the list of rules together, he expressed worry about his ability to remember them and fear of the consequences if he broke one of the rules. He said that he was scared to go to school. To help him work through his anxiety, I made up some additional, silly rules, just for fun. Here are some examples: 1) It is forbidden to set fire to the school. 2) No child may drive a car to school. 3) No child may arrive at school naked. 4) It is forbidden to eat the books at school. Nicky laughed heartily while I stated these rules with mock seriousness. Afterwards, he felt more relaxed and confident about attending his new school (and he never broke any of the rules).

My son's laughter in this example was the key element that allowed him to release anxiety about breaking rules.

Bullying

Many children suffer from teasing and bullying at school. In addition to addressing these issues with the school staff, you can also help your child at home. Here's an experience with my son.

> At six years of age, Nicky told me that a mean child at school had purposely knocked down his block tower. I used symbolic play to help him work though this experience. I built a miniature block tower with small blocks and used a monster puppet as the bully who knocked it down. Nicky laughed and eagerly joined in the play, wanting to play the part of the bully. After engaging in this activity several times, he felt more confident about going to school.

To help an older child who has been bullied, you can invite her to draw a picture of the bully or make a clay model of him, and then let her destroy the picture or clay model. But don't let this activity become too serious. Encourage laughter by playing the part of the bully and loudly expressing agony while your child destroys the symbolic representation. Your child will probably laugh if you do so, and this will help her release tensions and anger.

"Mean" teachers

Your child may find school stressful and blame her teachers even when they are highly qualified and compassionate. The school setting itself may feel oppressive to your child. Perhaps she finds it hard to sit for long periods, feels bored, or finds that the teaching approach does not work well with her learning style. Perhaps the teacher didn't call on your child when her hand was raised, and she felt ignored. Maybe the teacher asked her to participate in a small group with children who were not her close friends. In all of these situations, your child may declare "I hate my teacher," or "my teacher is mean."

Your child needs you to be her ally, and will not feel supported or understood if you defend her teacher's actions or tell her that she has a wonderful teacher (even though this may be true). If she perceives her teacher as mean, it's important to accept that feeling without judgment. Whatever the reason for your child's dislike of her teacher, you can help your child by engaging her in symbolic play with a school theme. Many children spontaneously play school games with friends or siblings, and this play allows them to process their school experiences. Your acceptance of your child's emotions and involvement in her play can accelerate her healing process.

When you play school games with your child, let her decide which role to play (teacher or student), and then let her take the lead. Your job is to prevent the play from becoming too serious. If your child plays the role of the student, you can turn the activity into a power-reversal game by role playing an incompetent teacher who makes obvious mistakes or a strict teacher who instills harsh discipline. If your child prefers to be the teacher, you can role play a rebellious child who then submits (in an exaggerated way) to adult authority when the teacher corrects or punishes her. If you keep the play silly and fun, your child will use the situation to release tensions through laughter.

If your child is too old to play school games, you can invite her to draw a picture or make a clay model of the teacher, and then let her destroy it while you provide the sound effects of someone being tortured. This approach is similar to the one described above for coping with bullying.

You are not really criticizing the teacher or undermining the teacher's authority when you allow your child to show aggression toward a symbolic representation of her teacher or when you play the role of an incompetent or mean teacher. Your child needs to know that you are willing to acknowledge and accept *all* of her emotions. If symbolically attacking her teacher at home helps her release stress or anger, then that is what she needs to do. With this approach, your child will process whatever stress she felt at school, whether it was the teacher's fault or not. Your child will return to school feeling understood and more confident, and may even surprise you later on by telling you that her teacher isn't so bad after all!

Note: For tips on helping your children with homework stress, see Part 2, Chapter 9. For tips on preparing your child for a new school or an upcoming test, see Part 3, Chapter 9.

Playful activities to help children cope with school stress

- Nonsense play (ex: suggest ridiculous school rules)

- Power-reversal games (ex: school games in which the parent plays the role of an incompetent or mean teacher)

- Symbolic play with toys and themes relating to school stress (ex: child plays role of a bully or destroys a clay model of a bully or teacher)

Chapter 8

Phobias and Anxieties

WHEN CHILDREN FEEL frightened, they sometimes become clingy, whiny, stubborn, and uncooperative. Frightened children also resist separation, sleep badly, or act aggressively. Their ability to learn, grow, and connect lovingly with others is hampered. If you take steps to help your children overcome their fears, their behavior will improve, and your entire family's stress level will probably decrease.

Children's fears have two major sources. *Developmental fears* can arise because of a child's growing awareness of death combined with a vivid imagination, whereas *traumatic fears* can occur following traumatic experiences. You can help your children overcome both kinds of fears through specific forms of play.

Developmental fears

At around three years of age, many children become aware of death, both their own and that of their parents. This awareness of mortality can lead to feelings of vulnerability and new fears. Typical fears include a fear of the dark, bathtubs, toilets, animals, and imaginary monsters. These early childhood fears can last until the age of eight years, or sometimes longer.

Symbolic play with props or themes relating to the child's fear is especially effective. In the following example, a mother reported the use of symbolic play with her three-year-old son who developed a fear of snakes.

Eric had the chicken pox just before his third birthday. That's when his fear of snakes began. I don't know if it was coincidental, or if it had something to do with the itchiness of the chicken pox. One evening, he thought he saw snakes on the floor. Then he said that they were on me too! It was almost like a hallucination. His fear would reappear in the evenings, especially when he was really tired. Sometimes he woke up in the night and started imagining snakes. This went on for months. His older brother was fascinated with cobras at the time, and Eric was also interested in them, so he knew a lot about snakes. I tried to get him to laugh. We made snakes out of play dough, and we created snake families. We had great fun cutting them up with a knife and laughing about them. We also played with plastic snakes and pretended that we were afraid of them. His fear gradually subsided.

The following example illustrates the use of symbolic play with my daughter to help her overcome a fear of spiders. The play then evolved into a power-reversal game in which I faked fright.

At four years of age, Sarah developed a fear of spiders. To help her overcome this fear, I played a game with her in which I tickled her arm or face with my finger and told her teasingly, "There's a spider crawling on you!" This always brought peals of laughter. Then she wanted to do it to me, so we took turns playing this spider game. When she walked her fingers on me like a spider, I pretended to be very frightened. After playing this game several times, she no longer panicked when she saw a spider.

My son enjoyed the following power-reversal game when he developed a fear of certain animals.

At three years of age, Nicky developed a fear of all animals (real or imaginary) that eat people, including sharks, lions, tigers, and dragons. He refused to look at books that featured them. However, he loved pretending to be a tiger while chasing me around the house. He laughed heartily when I faked fear and ran away. When I let him catch me, he pretended to eat me with much glee.

A mother described the following power-reversal game that she played with her two sons and their friends.

I often played an outdoor game called "the bad witch" with my sons and their friends when they were between four and eight years old. I pretended to be a hungry witch who wanted to catch all the children and put them in my soup pot. But I could catch them only when they came out of their safe house in order to collect treasures. When I managed to catch one of them, I put him in a make-believe pot and then continued to chase the others. A child who was caught could be freed if another child touched him. As the children liberated each other when I wasn't looking, I pretended to become increasingly discouraged and tired. By the end of the game, the children were all free, and they collected all the treasures. As for me, I rolled on the ground, famished and in despair because there were no children left in my pot, and I didn't have anything to eat. They loved this game and laughed a lot whenever we played it.

When you first introduce a symbolic activity or power-reversal game to trigger your children's fears, it's important to begin gradually and be sensitive to your children's reactions. Follow their lead. They will let you know if the delicate balance between feelings of fear and safety is not right.

Children seem to know intuitively how to create a therapeutic activity for themselves, and they sometimes invent their own games to help conquer their fears. The following examples describe two games that my daughter invented.

At six years of age, Sarah created a game called "the danger house." She stood on top of a small play house in our back yard and announced that she offered a rescue service. First she wanted me to pretend to be a little girl who had fallen into a pond and couldn't swim. She rushed over to me and pulled me out with a stick. Then I had to climb up into a tree and pretend to be stuck up there. She arrived with a rope to help me down. Then she instructed me to sit in a lawn chair and pretend it was a burning house. She brought an imaginary trampoline and asked me to jump to safety. Finally, she announced that I was surrounded by poisonous snakes, and she proceeded to rescue me by shooting them with a stick.

At eight years of age, Sarah made up another interesting game, which she called "the dark game." When it was dark in the evening, she switched off the light and asked me to hide quietly somewhere in a room while she made noise to prevent herself from hearing where I hid. Then she searched for me by feeling her way around the room. When she found me, I was supposed to say "boo!" This made her laugh, of course. After we had played this game several times, I asked her why she liked it. She immediately explained, "It helps me get over my fear of the dark."

By acting out these imaginary scenes, my daughter worked through some of her fears. I felt that my participation greatly contributed to the therapeutic effectiveness. So if your children invite you to play these kinds of games with them, try to find the time (and energy) to do so.

Between the ages of eight and twelve years, children often ponder the concept of death and the whole meaning of life with a new level of awareness. A fear of death can reappear during this developmental stage. Contrary to the irrational fears of early childhood, these middle childhood fears can be quite realistic.

Play that allows children to laugh about the topic of death can be useful. The following example illustrates my use of silly nonsense play with my son who expressed a fear of death.

> At ten years of age, Nicky seemed preoccupied with the concept of death and war, and he frequently asked about these topics with questions such as "what's the point of living if I'm just going to die some day?" and "will I have to fight in a war when I'm grown up?" I tried to answer his questions and reassure him as best I could. But his obsession and anxiety did not decrease, and he had two nightmares about death, which caused him to cry. In addition to supporting his need to cry, I also used a playful approach to help him through this difficult period. One evening at bedtime, I said to him, "Now what's that D-word that you're afraid of?" (referring to the word, *death*, but not saying it). "Is it Dandelions? Is it Doorknobs? Is it Dinosaurs?" He began to laugh and then joined in the game of naming objects starting with the letter D. Together, we pretended to be afraid of those objects. After playing the game a few more times at bedtime, his obsession with death decreased.

When my daughter had a nightmare, I used a similar approach, as described in the following example.

> After a day of sledding down a hill at eight years of age, Sarah awakened in the night after a nightmare about sliding down a hill and dropping off a cliff. She cried a little but then stopped crying. However, she said that she was still too frightened to go back to asleep. I told her, "That was a very scary dream. Did you think you were going to die?" She replied angrily, "Don't use that word. It's too scary." So I revised my question by avoiding the word "die" but using a word that rhymed with it, "Did you think you were going to *have some pie?*" At this, she laughed heartily and continued to laugh each time I repeated it. After a few minutes of this game, she lay down and fell asleep immediately.

Traumatic fears

In addition to the normal developmental fears during childhood, specific traumatic events can also cause fears. Just as with developmental fears, symbolic play can be highly effective in helping children overcome traumatic fears. One form of symbolic play is role playing. If your child has a post-traumatic fear, you can help him heal by acting out the traumatic incident in a playful way, thereby desensitizing him to the trauma.

A mother reported the following example to me.

When my daughter was six years old, we lived in a small town. She and a neighbor child usually walked home from school together. One day, however, the other child was not at school. As my daughter walked home alone, some teenagers signaled for her to come over to their car. Instead, she dropped her lunch box on the street and ran home as fast as she could. After that incident, she was terrified of going out in public even if we were with her. While walking down Main Street holding hands with both her Dad and me, she would cry and beg us to take her home. No amount of reassurance or talking on our part would alleviate her fear, so we sought help from the local mental health office. The psychologist talked with us all for a few minutes to hear about the precipitating incident, and he chatted with her about her fear that the teens wanted to kidnap her. He then suggested a family role play activity in which all family members (including us, our daughter, and her two older brothers) should take turns playing the different roles of the child and the teens. He encouraged us to "ham it up" and have fun with the role playing. Our whole family eagerly implemented this suggestion. We played through the incident once or twice a day for one week. When we went back to our next appointment, we were able to report that all her fears were totally gone, and we had our happy-go-lucky daughter back! From that point on, and for the rest of her schooling, she continued to walk home from school without an adult, and she had no further recurrence of fear.

In the following example from one of my clients, a child developed a fear after hearing about a traumatic event that happened to someone else. The mother helped him overcome the fear with symbolic play and also power-reversal play.

Victor, age five, developed a fear of policemen and death after hearing about a family whose adult son was shot by a policeman. He asked constantly if he and his brother were going to get killed, and he frequently pointed his fingers at his mother, saying "bang, bang." I suggested make-believe play with a policeman uniform and hat. I also suggested a power-reversal game in which the mother should put on a mock display of fear and fall onto the floor when her son aimed his fingers at her and pretended to shoot. I explained that Victor could resolve his fear through these games, provided that he laughed.

Children can become traumatized by seemingly minor events, such as a teacher who corrects the child's performance. Sensitive children sometimes interpret any correction as criticism and begin to feel anxious about making mistakes. In the following example, I used both symbolic play and power-reversal play to address a child's performance anxiety.

Six-year-old Wendy had taken an art class in which the teacher pointed out mistakes in her drawings. Since then, Wendy was hesitant to draw and afraid to try new things. She had begun to read, but refused to do so for fear of making a mistake, and she became upset and easily lost confidence when she made mistakes in other activities (for example, an online phonics program). Her mother brought her for a play-coaching session. After an initial period of nondirective child-centered play and a power-reversal game with her mother, I told Wendy that I was going to teach a new game to her, her mother, and a stuffed lion. I warned her ahead of time that the lion had a hard time with new games and usually made lots of mistakes. I gave Wendy a set of eight differently-shaped blocks and placed a matching set of blocks in front of the lion. I told Wendy to build something with her blocks, and I said that we would see if the lion could copy her. After Wendy built a simple block construction, I played the role of the lion and had him make a mistake while trying to copy her construction. Wendy showed him the correct way to do it. We repeated the activity several times, and Wendy corrected the lion each time he made a mistake. Then I role played the lion having a temper tantrum because he was so frustrated. During the lion's tantrum, Wendy giggled. Then she wanted to play the role of the lion and enjoyed having him make mistakes and throw tantrums. We changed roles several times among the three of us. At one point, Wendy told the lion reassuringly, "Everybody makes mistakes." We continued this activity for about thirty minutes until she wanted to play something else. After the session, Wendy asked her mother to buy a toy lion exactly like the one we had used in the play session! The following week, she told her mother, "I'm the total opposite of the lion. I'm not afraid to make mistakes." Her mother also noticed a change in Wendy's attitude while using an online phonics program. When she made a mistake and the computerized voice announced "incorrect," Wendy replied to the voice by saying "so what!" Before the play session, she had become upset and intimidated each time the voice corrected her. A few weeks later, she created a coloring book and confidently announced that she wanted to publish it!

By using a playful context to bring up this child's anxiety about making mistakes, we helped her gain self-confidence. Her desire for a toy lion similar to the one we had used during the play indicated that she wanted to continue the same kind of play at home.

To conclude this chapter, children's fears can represent a normal developmental stage or can arise following a traumatic event. In both cases, these fears can lead to behavior problems and stress for the entire family. You can help your children overcome fears by implementing specific forms of play. However, if your children's fears interfere with their ability to function normally at home or at school, or if their post-traumatic fears last more than a month after a traumatic incident, I recommend seeking professional advice.

Playful activities to help children cope with phobias and anxiety

- Symbolic play with props or themes relating to the phobia/anxiety (ex: clay snakes, making mistakes)

- Power-reversal games involving the child's fear (ex: tigers, monsters, witches, policemen).

- Nonsense play in which you exaggerate the fear or make it silly (ex: pretending to be afraid of the letter "D" for a child afraid of death)

Chapter 9

Preparation for Difficult Events

CHILDREN'S LIVES ARE FULL OF difficult events, such as the first day of school, a medical procedure, the birth of a sibling, or a move to a new home. Sometimes children show their anxiety about upcoming events through difficult behaviors. They may become clingy, whiny, demanding, uncooperative, obnoxious, or aggressive. Some children may begin to act like a baby when they face a future challenge.

One of the best ways to prepare your child for a difficult event is to introduce symbolic play with props or themes relating to the event. This approach is similar to the one described in preceding chapters for helping children cope with trauma that has already occurred (such as natural disasters or medical procedures) and also for miscellaneous fears and phobias.

The following example illustrates the use of symbolic play to prepare a child for riding on a school bus.

Five-year-old Anne-Marie knew that she would have to take a school bus for the first time when she started attending a new school in September. In July, she began to show signs of stress and repeatedly asked questions about the school bus. At my suggestion, the parents obtained a large cardboard box (from a new refrigerator), cut a door and windows in it, and painted it yellow (like the school bus). Anne-Marie and her parents spent many hours during the summer playing with the cardboard school bus and pretending to drive it to school. On the first day of school, Anne-Marie confidently climbed into the school bus when it arrived to pick her up in front of her home.

Sometimes children invent their own symbolic play in preparation for something new. The following example illustrates how my son found a way to rehearse the first day of nursery school.

> The day before starting nursery school at three years of age, Nicky invented a school game with his imaginary babies (which often entered his make-believe play). He pretended to bring them to school, go to a restaurant without them, and then pick them up. He brought them to me and asked them how they had liked school. He obviously wanted me to speak for them, so I pretended to be his babies and told Nicky everything they had done at school. He wanted to repeat this game several times. Then he decided that he was the daddy and I was the child, and he pretended to drive me to school. He buckled me into an imaginary car seat and drove me to school in an imaginary car. On the first day of school, Nicky felt eager and confident.

Role playing can be a useful technique for preparing children for medical procedures. A mother reported the following incident to me.

> When Caitlin was three years old, she fell forward off of the living room couch and hit her face on our wooden coffee table. The point of impact was her tooth and lip, making for quite a bloody injury, which resulted in a big cry. Later, we were told she would have to have this tooth extracted because it had died at the root, and an abscess was growing above it. My husband and I both planned to be with her for the extraction, which would be done under local anesthesia. To prepare her for this procedure, I set up her small dollhouse dolls and said, "Let's play going to the dentist to

have your tooth taken out." Caitlin selected dolls to represent each person, including herself. The first time through, I played all of the parts except for hers. While acting out the dentist's role, I explained what was going to happen and showed her the tools. This was funny, as the tools were huge compared to the little dolls! Then we role played the extraction, starting with the injection to numb her mouth. She loved this activity and wanted to do it over and over. The first time we role played the procedure, she was wide-eyed and attentive, but each time we repeated it, she became more active and engaged. And the more we played, the more she laughed. Eventually, she acted out the part of the dentist. Playing this game took the anxiety out of waiting for the procedure, and it prepared her for the experience. When the day of the extraction arrived, Caitlin was calm, relaxed, and cooperative. She did not cry or protest. In fact, she seemed to have no trauma around the extraction at all. The dentist was impressed that such a young child could be so calm.

Children sometimes think of their own creative ways to overcome anxiety before a frightening event such as a medical procedure. A mother reported the following example to me.

When Nancy was four years old, she had to have her adenoids removed. After our pre-operation visit to the surgeon, Nancy felt anxious about the anesthesia. I explained how they would put her to sleep, but that didn't seem to help. She still felt uneasy about the process. A couple of days later, we were drawing and coloring in bed before we went to sleep, and suddenly she lay down flat on her back, put my hand over her nose and mouth, began to breath in and out very dramatically, and then pretended to fall asleep. A few seconds later, she began to laugh hysterically! She did this a few more times and then made *me* lie down while she covered my nose and mouth with her hand. I pretended to fall asleep, and then we both started laughing a lot. We played this game until we fell asleep (for real), and when we woke up the next morning, she started playing it again. She played this game in different forms until the hour before her surgery. She even got the nurses and surgeon to play with her! Nancy was relaxed, happy, and in great spirits before her surgery, and she healed quickly afterwards with no emotional issues. The nurses and the surgeon even commented on how relaxed she was and how easy it was to be with her and communicate with her. They noticed a significant difference in my daughter compared to other children they had treated.

Nonsense play can help children who feel anxious about an upcoming performance, such as a school test, dance show, piano recital, or theater performance. You can encourage your child to make intentional mistakes. For example, ask her to purposely give incorrect answers when you quiz her, play the wrong notes on the piano, do the wrong dance steps, or recite the memorized lines incorrectly. Encourage your child to be silly and to laugh. This activity will help reduce her anxiety. The expression "bad rehearsal, good performance" has some truth in it because the performer has already made mistakes and is therefore unlikely to make them again. Play allows the young performer or test taker to make all possible mistakes ahead of time while reducing tensions through the healing mechanism of laughter.

Some children can benefit from regression play when they feel anxious about an upcoming event, such as the birth of a sibling or a move to a new home. Often, these children will indicate this need by initiating baby play themes. Here is an example from my son.

At four years of age, Nicky learned that I was expecting a baby. In addition to asking lots of questions, he also enjoyed pretending to be a baby himself. He crawled around and pretended that he didn't know how to talk. I pretended to change his diaper and nurse him. This regression play may have been a way to reassure himself that he could still be a baby if he wanted to and that I would still be available to take care of him after the birth of his sister.

The following example from one of my clients illustrates the need for regression play in a six-year-old child.

> When six-year-old Richard's family began making plans to move to a new home where Richard would have his own room, he began showing signs of anxiety. He stated that he didn't want to grow up, and he frequently used baby talk at home. I advised the mother to encourage baby play and treat her son like a baby (holding, rocking, feeding, etc.), in a fun, playful way (without teasing).

This child's desire to act like a baby in this example indicated that he needed to experience more of the baby stage before he could feel confident about the upcoming change.

By playing with your children in these various ways, you can prepare them emotionally for life's inevitable difficulties. This play and laughter will reduce their anxiety about upcoming events, and they will become more cooperative and easier to live with.

Playful activities to help children prepare for difficult events

- Symbolic play with props or themes relating to the upcoming event (ex: school games, doctor play)

- Nonsense play in which you encourage the child to make mistakes about the upcoming event (such as a test or performance).

- Regression games

Chapter 10

Parental Anger

YOUR OWN ANGER can be a source of stress for your child. Most parents become impatient with their children from time to time. Some parents lose control and do things that they later regret, such as speaking harshly to their children or even hitting them. When this occurs, children feel terrified, confused, and abandoned. Normally, children use their parents as a safe base when they feel frightened or hurt, seeking comfort in their parents' arms. But when the parents themselves cause the distress, the children have nobody to comfort them and no place to feel safe.

Parental anger can occur for two reasons. One reason involves events in your present life. Perhaps you feel stressed because of difficulties related to work, relationships, health, or money. Or perhaps you have unmet needs for rest, leisure activities, or time away from your children.

The second source of parental anger is your own childhood. Your children's behavior can trigger your own unresolved childhood issues. Perhaps your son's crying reminds you of your father's anger when you cried as a child. Perhaps your daughter's demanding behavior reminds you of the fact that your own mother never gave you the attention you needed. When your son hits his little sister, you may be reminded of an older brother who used to beat you up. If you had an abusive childhood or suffered from unmet needs, your anger will probably be triggered frequently, especially if you have not had an opportunity to resolve your childhood traumas through therapy.

These childhood triggers often occur at an unconscious level, so you may not be aware of the connection with your childhood. When these triggers occur, the part of your brain that allows you to respond appropriately and lovingly to your children shuts down. You become preoccupied primarily with your own survival, as if you were once again a powerless child. This shift in your brain function can cause you to respond to your children in hurtful ways, leading to a rupture in your loving bond with them.

Children respond to these moments of disconnection in a variety of ways. Some children become demanding, obnoxious, or even aggressive. The situation can quickly escalate into a vicious cycle of mutual anger and hurt feelings. Other children become quiet and withdrawn, retreating in fear.

Luckily, you can repair these moments of disconnection. When you find yourself caught up in anger at your child, remove yourself from the situation and do whatever it takes to regain your composure and inner peace. You can take a bathroom break or breathe deeply and count to ten. Perhaps you can scream into a pillow or call a trusted friend and share your feelings. Although your child may feel temporarily abandoned, it's important to attend to your feelings so you don't continue to express anger at him.

When you reach a calmer state, try to re-establish a loving connection with your child. Depending on your child's age, an apology may be appropriate, as well as an explanation that your behavior had nothing to do with him. If he says "I hate you" or "you're mean," accept his statements by replying, for example: "I can understand why you feel that way. I know I hurt your feelings and frightened you. I shouldn't have yelled at you." If your child cries, try to be supportive of his need to release feelings through tears.

You can also engage your child in several forms of play to further repair the ruptured bond between you. Power-reversal play is a wonderful way to help your child heal from the trauma of your own anger. Here is an example from a parent-child play session that I coached.

Three-year-old Manuel had been expelled from nursery school because of aggressive behavior toward other chil-

dren. His mother, Michelle, had been authoritarian and punitive with him in the past, and she had frequently lost her
temper and yelled at him. She had started therapy and was
making efforts to switch to a less authoritarian approach to
discipline. Nevertheless, Manuel still had a lot of pent-up
anger, which his mother felt was a direct result of her for-
mer approach to discipline. We began the play session by
letting Manuel choose what to play with from a variety of
toys. He chose to play with some small wooden blocks. After about one minute, he began to throw the blocks angrily
at his mother. This was a cue for us to begin a power-reversal game, so I gave him a pillow and invited him to knock
his mother down with it. He did this gleefully while laughing heartily. Michelle played her part well by dramatically
falling on the floor. We spent the rest of the hour playing
several more kinds of power-reversal games. Manuel buried
his mother under pillows, locked her up behind chairs and
pretended to throw the key away, frightened his mother
with plastic bugs, snakes, and a crocodile puppet, and gave
her imaginary shots using a doctor kit. We encouraged this
play and kept him laughing for about 45 minutes. Toward
the end, his play suddenly switched, and a more gentle and
compassionate part of him began to emerge. He pretended
that his mother was sick while he used props from the doctor kit to lovingly take care of her. I encouraged Michelle
to continue playing power-reversal games at home. A few
weeks later, she reported to me that Manuel's behavior had
completely changed, and he was no longer aggressive with
other children.

With older children, power-reversal games can take the form of a
board game in which you let your child win and then complain bitterly about losing. This activity will help your child dominate you
symbolically, which is a wonderful contradiction to your previous
angry outburst.

Symbolic play with puppets or stuffed animals can help, especially with younger children. Using the toys as props, you can role play the angry scene between you and your child. For example, act out a scene in which a child bear does something that triggers a mama (or papa) bear's anger, which in turn causes the child bear to become hurt and frightened. Explain that the mama bear is not being a good mama at that moment. This symbolic play will allow your child to make sense of what happened. He may want to become actively involved in the play. If so, encourage him to play the role of the child bear and to tell the mama bear that she shouldn't get angry. You can also switch roles and let him play the role of the parent.

You can also use nonsense play to help your child cope with your anger. For example, you can exaggerate the emotions in a silly way and act them out playfully with each other. A mother reported the following game.

> When Katie (age five) and I are angry with each other, we sometimes express ourselves in a physical way by having an imaginary cat fight, which allows us to release our aggressive energy with our arms, hands, and voices. When words just aren't enough, and I can see that Katie wants to express her anger, I encourage her by making a hissing sound like an angry cat, and I use my hands like cat paws. Katie sees this cue as permission to do the same, so we hiss at each other and lightly swat each other with our "paws" for a minute or two until we start to laugh. Then we talk about what made us mad and what we need to do next.

Older children may benefit by role playing the scene with you. To make it silly and funny, you can use role reversal. Invite your child to pretend to be you while you pretend to be him. Exaggerate what actually happened. The laughter during this nonsense play will help both of you release tensions and heal from the rupture in your relationship. You may also gain insight and perspective by seeing how your child imitates your behavior.

Activities with body contact can also help repair a ruptured bond. If your child refuses to let you hug him, or if he resists snuggling close to you, you can incorporate touch into playful activities. The following suggestions might work: a hand clapping game, doctor play, a piggy-back ride, or a power-reversal game in which he must put his arms around you to prevent you from escaping.

Cooperative games are useful as well because they will remind your child that you are his ally rather than his opponent. Other cooperative activities, such as making music together, can also be beneficial.

You will probably experience many moments of disconnection and repair as your children grow, and each moment of repair will strengthen your relationship with them. However, if you find that you are unable to repair the damage done by your anger, or if the moments of disconnection outnumber the moments or repair, I advise you to seek therapy for yourself. If you can take steps to make connections with your own childhood and heal from your childhood traumas, you will probably find that your patience with your children increases, as well as your ability to repair your relationship through play.

Playful activities to help children heal from your own anger

- Power-reversal games

- Symbolic play with puppets or stuffed animals to re-enact the fight you had with your child

- Nonsense play in which you use silliness, exaggeration, or role reversal to re-enact the fight

- Activities with body contact

- Cooperative games and activities

Summary Charts of the Nine Forms of Attachment Play

Guidelines for nondirective child-centered play

• Provide a variety of toys and materials (building materials, dolls, doll house, puppets, clay, dress-up clothes, art supplies, small figures, animals, vehicles, etc).

• Sit near your child (on the floor, if possible) and give him your full, relaxed attention. Make arrangements so you won't have to answer the telephone or attend to other children.

• Be nondirective. Let your child lead the way and play with whatever he wants.

• Enter into the play if your child invites you.

• Comment on your child's play, but refrain from analyzing or teaching.

• Be permissive, but establish safety limits, as needed (ex: "I can't let you throw blocks at the window.").

• Schedule half an hour of this play with each child, at least once a week (or more).

Guidelines for symbolic play
with specific props or themes
(relating to trauma)

Child-initiated

• When your child engages in any play that resembles a previous traumatic experience, seize the opportunity to encourage the symbolic play and pay attention to her.

Adult-initiated

• Select a time when you are both calm and rested. Make sure your child feels safe and comfortable with you.

• Engage your child in play with a toy or an activity that contains an element of the trauma (ex: toy cars, ambulance, fire truck, doctor kit, teddy bear family).

• Encourage fantasy play, talking, and laughter.

• Carefully observe your child's behavior. If she is eager to play, continue the activity. If she withdraws, loses interest, or shows signs of distress, stop or modify the activity.

Guidelines for contingency play

Basic contingency play

• Wait until your child initiates an action (ex: throws an object on the floor, pokes your nose).

• Make a funny sound or movement that is *contingent* on your child's action (ex: stick your tongue out each time your child pokes your nose).

• Repeat your action each time the child repeats the initial action.

• Encourage laughter.

• (More advanced): Introduce variations with several different contingencies (ex: piggy-back rides in which your child gives you movement commands by tapping different parts of your body).

Imitative contingency play

• When your child makes a sound, movement, or expression, imitate him playfully.

• Continue to imitate him each time he repeats the sound or movement.

• For an older child, suggest a traditional imitation game (such as "Follow the leader" or "Simon says") and let him be the leader.

Guidelines for nonsense play

Child-initiated

• When your child purposely does something "wrong" (ex: puts socks on her hands), join her playfully while encouraging her to be silly and make other mistakes.

• Encourage laughter.

Adult-initiated

• (For discipline conflicts): Exaggerate a behavior or conflict so it becomes ridiculous, or invent a silly game.

• (For fears): Suggest a game in which you both pretend to be frightened of something trivial (ex: the sound "S" for a child who is terrified of snakes).

• Encourage laughter.

• Ensure that your child does not feel teased or ridiculed.

Guidelines for separation games

• Create a temporary separation with your child by playing peek-a-boo, hide-and-seek, or chasing games.

• Find each other and re-establish visual and/or physical connection.

• Encourage laughter.

• Don't remain hidden or separated too long if your child shows signs of distress.

Guidelines for power-reversal games

• Pretend to be weak, frightened, clumsy, or stupid.

• Let your child "knock" you down, frighten you, catch you, make you wait, or beat you in a game (or use puppets to act out these behaviors).

• Encourage laughter.

• Establish safety limits during play, as needed, and make it clear that your child should not try these activities with other people who might not understand.

Guidelines for regression games

Child-initiated

• Your child pretends to be a baby or a younger child.

• Treat him like a baby in a playful way. Play baby games or initiate a nurturing activity (ex: feeding, holding, rocking, singing).

Adult-initiated

• Initiate baby games (ex: "this little piggy," "pat-a-cake," or simple contingency play).

• Initiate a nurturing activity (ex: feeding, holding, rocking, singing).

Guidelines for activities
with body contact

• Frequently hold and cuddle your child.

• Engage your child in playful activities involving touch
  (ex: piggy-back rides, dancing to music together).

• Look for ways to incorporate touch into sports, games,
  and other activities.

• When your child initiates touch, don't push her away.
  If she clings to you, make a game of it (ex: pretend that
  you are glued together).

• Be respectful of your child's boundaries if she doesn't
  want to be held or touched, but look for playful ways to
  connect physically (ex: a hand-clapping game or hiding
  toys in your sleeve).

Guidelines for cooperative
games and activities

• Engage your child in cooperative activities (ex: singing,
  cooking, crafts).

• Play cooperative games (ex: build a cooperative block
  tower, tell a cooperative story).

• Look for cooperative board games or modify traditional
  ones.

• Modify traditional sports to make them non-competitive
  (ex: cooperative tennis).

• Emphasize having fun and reaching a common goal
  rather than winning or losing.

Research Basis for Attachment Play

Brief overview of attachment theory

John Bowlby, a British psychiatrist and psychoanalyst, was the first person to use the term *attachment* to refer to a child's bond with his mother. He considered mother-child social interaction to be an important factor that fostered healthy attachment (Bowlby, 1988). Psychologists now use the term attachment to refer to a child's bond with both parents, as well as to significant others who are emotionally close to the child and intimately involved in caregiving.

Mary Ainsworth investigated attachment behavior in infants and young children. She found a clear-cut relationship between the quality of the mother-infant interaction during the first year after birth and a baby's attachment behavior at one year of age. She conducted home observations of mothers with their infants and also did laboratory observations of the babies when they were one year old. She discovered that babies whose mothers had been consistently responsive to them during the first year were securely attached by one year of age. Those whose mothers tended to ignore or reject their infants, or who were inconsistent in responding to them, were insecurely attached (Ainsworth *et al.*, 1971).

A child's healthy, secure attachment to a loving, responsive parent is vital for optimal development. Bowlby discovered through his research and clinical work that lack of maternal responsiveness, as well as prolonged separations between mother and child early in a child's life, could not only disrupt the normal attachment process but also lead to severe negative consequences later in life (Bowlby, 1982).

A longitudinal study of children from infancy to adulthood has confirmed Bowlby's observations. Children who lacked a secure attachment to their mothers as infants had more conduct disorders and anxiety disorders later on. Children with secure attachment histories fared much better. They were less aggressive, less anxious, and more confident. They also had more friends later on and were rated by their teachers as more competent (Sroufe *et al.*, 2005).

Research on therapeutic play (general)

Therapists have recognized the healing effects of play for decades. Specific forms of play therapy can help children who suffer from a variety of emotional, behavioral, and neurological problems, including attachment disorder, post-traumatic stress, fears and anxiety, aggressive behavior, ADHD, and autism (Reddy *et al.*, 2005). Play-based interventions can also be beneficial in medical situations, such as preparing children for surgery (Li & Lopez, 2008).

Parental involvement in play therapy treatment increases the likelihood of successful outcomes. One study found that eight weeks of play therapy training for parents and teachers significantly reduced problem behaviors in preschool children who were at risk for mental health problems (Draper *et al.*, 2009). For child trauma survivors, researchers found that parental involvement in play therapy also contributed to the success of the therapy (Reddy *et al.*, 2005).

Research on the benefits of laughter

Researchers have identified both physiological and psychological benefits of laughter for people of all ages. It can improve immune function, increase pain tolerance, decrease the stress response, and reduce anxiety, thereby restoring a person's physiological balance following frightening or traumatic events (Bennett & Lengacher, 2006a, 2006b, 2008, 2009; Wilkins & Eisenbraun, 2009).

Laughter-promoting activities (such as clowns) with children in hospitals have shown that humor and laughter can reduce anxiety and pain while promoting healing (Fernandes & Arriaga, 2010).

In addition to the therapeutic effects of laughter, fostering a sense of humor in children may help improve their social competence, popularity, and adaptability (Semrud-Klikeman & Glass, 2010).

Research on nondirective child-centered play

Nondirective child-centered play is based on Virginia Axline's play therapy model, which builds on Carl Rogers' *client-centered therapy* (Axline, 1969; Rogers, 1951). Axline made the assumption that if we allow children to play freely with a variety of materials, and if an adult shows interest, warmth, empathy, and acceptance, the child will use the situation to release blocked emotions and reduce inner conflicts (Axline, 1969). Axline recommends materials that inspire children to imagine, create, and build. Effective materials include blocks, dolls, a doll house, puppets, sand, clay, dress-up clothes, art supplies, small figures, animals, and vehicles. During nondirective play therapy sessions, children often select toys and create scenes that are symbolic of their experiences of trauma.

Specially trained paraprofessionals have used nondirective child-centered play therapy successfully in school settings with children showing emotional or behavioral problems, and with children who have difficulty adjusting to the school environment. Controlled studies with children between the ages of four and nine years have shown positive results. After a semester of weekly child-centered play sessions with trained paraprofessionals, children become less aggressive, have fewer learning difficulties, and show more social competence (Johnson *et al.*, 2005).

Therapists have used nondirective child-centered play therapy successfully with child victims of domestic violence (Kot & Tyndall-Lind, 2005). This form of play was also used successfully with children affected by the Oklahoma City bombing, and some children needed only one to three sessions for full recovery (Webb, 2001).

Some therapists have developed an approach called *filial therapy* in which they train parents to facilitate nondirective play therapy sessions with their own children. Research studies have shown that this kind of play between parents and children can help children work through feelings resulting from trauma and also resolve problems with behavior or relationships (Rye, 2008; VanFleet *et al.*, 2005).

Research on symbolic play with specific props or themes

Symbolic play with specific props or themes is more directive than the nondirective play described in the previous section. The therapist provides toys or activities that are symbolic of the child's struggles or past traumas (such as accidents, hospitalization, abuse, or natural disasters). This kind of play has two different theoretical rationales, one from behavioral psychology, and the other from psychoanalytic theory.

According to the behavioral model, in order to heal from trauma, children must be reminded of the trauma in a safe context in order to become desensitized to it. We store traumatic memories in the limbic system, which is not the same area of the brain where we store positive or neutral memories (Debiec & LeDoux, 2006; Tronel & Alberini, 2007). In the limbic system, these traumatic memories have direct connections with the system that triggers our fight or flight response. In the past, this quick mechanism allowed humans to survive by avoiding life-threatening dangers.

Sometimes, however, the traumatic memories fail to decrease over time and no longer serve a useful purpose, yet they continue to trigger the body's alarm system when something triggers a memory of the original trauma. When symptoms of panic last more than a month after a traumatic event, psychologists use the term *post-traumatic stress disorder* (PTSD).

Therapeutic approaches that expose people to the very items that frighten them are called *exposure therapies* because desensitization occurs during repeated exposure to the trauma triggers (Jacob & Pelham, 2005). Play therapy with props or themes related to the trauma can provide desensitization for traumatized children (Gaensbauer & Siegel, 1995). For example, children who have been hospitalized can become desensitized to the trauma while repeatedly reenacting their frightening experience with props, such as a doctor kit, dolls, and a doll bed. In order for this kind of therapy to be effective, the children must feel safe and must understand that the trauma will not recur.

The psychoanalytic model proposes a different theoretical rationale for the effectiveness of symbolic play therapy. Instead of emphasizing the desensitizing nature of symbolic play, trauma-focused psychoanalytic play therapists emphasize the importance of emotional expression (also called *catharsis*) (Astramovich, 1999). For example, a child who uses a toy syringe to give shots to the therapist may be expressing anger resulting from feelings of helplessness in the hospital. The therapist's ability to reflect and accept the child's emotions is considered a vital therapeutic component.

It's likely that both theoretical rationales for the effectiveness of symbolic play are valid. Children can become desensitized to trauma through exposure to trauma reminders during play, but it's possible that the desensitization will be effective and permanent only if the children also have the opportunity to express emotions with an empathic witness. Evidence for this theory comes from the observation that solitary post-traumatic play does not appear to have any therapeutic value for traumatized children. Children sometimes compulsively re-enact traumatic events through play but do not benefit from this solitary activity (Terr, 1983).

Therapists have developed a variety of therapeutic approaches for children, which provide both desensitization and emotional expression through the medium of symbolic play. An early form of symbolic play with children in the U.S. was called *release therapy* (Levy, 1938). The therapist provided the child with toys or play themes that were directly related to traumatic events in the child's life. A later term for a similar approach was *structured play therapy* (Hambridge, 1982). The terms *trauma-focused cognitive-behavioral therapy* and *post-traumatic play therapy* are now used for approaches that involve a similar focus (Reddy *et al.*, 2005).

Violet Oaklander developed a comprehensive *Gestalt therapy* approach for children, which uses the symbolic nature of toys and puppets as well as other representative activities, such as stories, artwork, and clay modeling. Her assumption is that the scenes children produce through play or artwork reflect what they are feeling. Her goal is to help children become aware of, and express, these emotions, which usually lie at the root of their behavioral and emotional problems (Oaklander, 1988, 2007).

Most of the documentation for the effectiveness of these

approaches comes from case studies rather than controlled experiments. Therapists have used forms of symbolic play successfully with children suffering from a variety of traumatic experiences, including physical and sexual abuse, natural disasters, parental divorce or death, terrorism, war, accidents, hospitalization, and surgery (Gaensbauer & Siegel, 1995; Oaklander, 2003; Saunders *et al.*, 2003; Shelby & Felix, 2005; Terr, 1992).

Even when a trauma occurs during infancy before children can talk, they can sometimes reenact it through play later on. For example, a 22-month-old girl reenacted with toy cars an auto accident that had occurred when she was nine months old. The mother was stunned by her daughter's accurate portrayal because the mother had never discussed the details of the accident with her (Gaensbauer, 1995). Another therapist reported that a 35-month-old girl spontaneously reenacted with dolls the sexual abuse she had experienced as an infant (Terr, 1988). There is even evidence that children can remember their own traumatic birth and reenact aspects of it later on (Emerson, 1989).

Therapists have also treated specific fears of unknown origin with symbolic play. For example, the use of clay (as a symbol for feces) has proven successful in treating children with constipation caused by fear of defecating (Feldman *et al.*, 1993).

Guided fantasy play (telling stories to help children feel powerful and strong) is especially beneficial for very ill children. As opposed to the forms of symbolic play described above, guided fantasy play for ill children does *not* incorporate traumatic elements (themes of illness, doctors, or hospitals), so it cannot be considered exposure therapy. The goal is to take the children's attention *away* from the feelings of pain and stress. Therapists who use guided fantasy play have found that the most helpful stories are those that incorporate elements of the child's life and that are filled with humor, adventure, surprises, and magic (Johnson & Kreimer, 2005).

Research on contingency play

There is a correlation between early contingency play and later attachment security. Four-months-old infants whose mothers made immediate responses to their vocalizations became securely attached later on, as opposed to infants who did not experience frequent contingent responsiveness (Bieglow *et al.*, 2010). When children have been abused or neglected, simple contingency games can help the children regain a sense of trust and control (Gunsberg, 1989).

Imitation games are one kind of contingency play. When a parent playfully imitates a baby's sounds, the baby experiences connection and emotional well-being because he feels himself reflected and valued by the parent (Siegel & Hartzell, 2003). Mutual imitations of facial expressions, sounds, and movements during infancy are also considered to play an important role in the development of intentionality, which is the ability to represent goals beyond the "here and now" of perception (Rochat, 2007).

Playful imitation games may also enhance the development of empathy and the interpretation of nonverbal cues in others (Meltzoff, 2002). Neuroscientists have discovered mirror neurons in the brain, which may facilitate this learning process. These mirror neurons help children feel the same emotions that others display through sounds, movements, or facial expressions. This mechanism could play a major role in the development of empathy and interpersonal social skills (Gallese, 2007).

Playful imitation of infants and young children therefore sets up the following series of events: (1) the child expresses something through sounds, facial expressions, or movements, (2) the parent imitates the child's sounds, expressions, and movements, (3) the child's mirror neurons cause her original feeling to be triggered and reinforced, (4) the child notices the similarity and feels validated, understood, and emotionally connected to the parent, and (5) the child learns to correctly interpret those cues in others.

Children suffering from autism appear to benefit greatly from imitative contingency play. These children have difficulty connecting socially with others, understanding other people's feelings or intentions, and engaging in symbolic play. However, they are often highly skilled at manipulating objects. Nobody knows the cause of autism, but one theory is a dysfunctional mirror neuron system (Williams, 2008). Studies have shown that the use of imitation can help facilitate social responsiveness in these children (Field *et al.*, 2001; Heimann *et al.*, 2006; Sanefuji & Ohgami, 2011).

The *Son-Rise* therapeutic approach to autism combines child-centered play with the adult's playful imitation of the autistic child's sounds and movements. This approach has proven to be effective in enhancing parent-child connection and reducing autistic behaviors in many children (Kaufman, 1994). Stanley Greenspan's *Floortime* approach for autistic children combines several forms of play, including child-centered play and contingency play, to create another comprehensive, play-based approach to autism (Greenspan & Wieder, 1997, 2006).

Research on nonsense play

Several therapists have incorporated nonsense play (humor based on exaggeration, mistakes, or general silliness) into their repertoire of tools for working with children (Goodheart, 1994; Cohen, 2001; Shelby & Felix, 2005). For example, in one approach for helping children with post-traumatic phobias, the child writes or draws each specific fear on an index card and rank orders them. The therapist then adds a few ridiculous items to the child's fear list, such as the child's own big toe, baby dolls, or French fries. Together, they engage in laughter sessions in which they act terrified of those silly items (Shelby & Felix, 2005). In a case study of a five-year-old child hospitalized for cancer, nonsense play helped decrease the child's anxiety during medical interventions (Frankenfield, 1996).

Research on separation games

The game of peek-a-boo has an interesting history. The words in old English originally meant "alive or dead." When you play peek-a-boo with your baby, it's as if you were asking "Am I alive or dead?" (Maurer, 1967). This game touches on deep emotional issues of separation and loss. Child psychoanalyst, Selma Fraiberg, was one of the first people to recognize the psychological importance of this game. She claimed that by repeating the disappearance and return of the attachment figure, the baby can overcome separation anxiety (Fraiberg, 1959).

Interestingly, only family-reared babies respond to the game of peek-a-boo. Babies raised in institutions (orphanages) do not laugh or react in any way during this game. They have no fear of separation because they have not formed an attachment to anybody (Provence & Lipton, 1962).

Separation games such as peek-a-boo and hide-and-seek are especially useful with children who have experienced a difficult separation or the loss of a parent. Children often initiate these separation games after such traumas. In one case study, a two-year-old girl whose mother had committed suicide played hide-and-seek with the therapist for several months. Through play, the child enacted her fear of abandonment and experienced reassurance each time the therapist found her (Ostler, 2011).

Research on power-reversal games

Active power-reversal games (such as pillow fights or roughhousing) are a form of play that researchers call *rough-and-tumble play*. Researchers have found that rat pups that lacked opportunities to engage in rough-and-tumble play developed numerous social problems as adults (Brown, 2009). In human children, rough-and-tumble play with peers is characterized by smiles and laughter, whereas true aggression is characterized by frowns and sometimes crying (Pellegrini & Perlmutter, 1988). It has been suggested that adults should engage children with conduct disorders in daily rough-and-tumble play sessions to help the children discriminate between real and mock fighting and also release excess energy (Pellegrini & Perlmutter, 1988). Other researchers have proposed that rough-and-tumble play may be a useful treatment for children with symptoms of ADHD (attention deficit hyperactivity disorder) (Panksepp, 2007).

Lawrence Cohen's therapeutic work with children includes numerous examples of active power-reversal play (Cohen 2001, DeBenedet & Cohen, 2010). He suggests that this kind of play helps boys and girls in different ways. Boys often struggle with the cultural expectations to be strong, competitive, and aggressive, whereas girls receive cultural messages to become passive and helpless. Active power-reversal play can help boys explore the themes of aggression and competition in the context of a warm connection with an adult. This kind of play can also empower girls by counteracting the cultural stereotypes of weak women (Cohen 2001).

Other therapists have incorporated less active forms of power-reversal play in their repertoire of techniques for empowering children and helping them work through anger or fear. One therapist pretended to be frightened when a four-year-old abused girl hid inside a large box and started growling like a lion (Gunsberg, 1989). Another therapist displayed mock terror in the context of a music therapy session when a timid, seven-year-old boy, who had been bullied at school, made a loud noise with two cymbals (Blend, 2009). Power-reversal play has also been done with puppets. During a therapy session with a ten-year-old girl who had suffered years of sexual and physical abuse, the therapist encouraged the girl to make her alligator puppet bite the therapist's shark puppet, which then "died" while making loud screeching and moaning sounds, much to the child's delight (Oaklander, 2003). During these successful therapy sessions, the children repeated their action several times and laughed heartily.

Research on regression games

Child psychologist, Bruno Bettelheim described a four-year-old girl who regressed when her mother became pregnant. The child started wetting her pants, crawling on all fours, and demanding to be fed with a bottle. This regression behavior lasted for a few months, and then the girl returned to more mature play in which she cared lovingly for a baby doll. Bettelheim claimed that the regression play helped the girl identify with the baby, and the doll play helped her identify with her mother. By playing both roles, she prepared herself for the upcoming birth of her sibling (Bettelheim, 1987).

A therapeutic approach called *Theraplay* makes extensive use of regression games (Booth & Jernberg, 2010). The basic idea is that parents can improve their connection with their children and help them heal from emotional problems by engaging them in forms of play that replicate the attuned, empathic, responsive, and playful interactions of a parent with her infant. This therapy is geared to the preverbal, social-emotional brain rather than to higher brain functions such as language or reasoning.

Theraplay sessions include simple activities, such as playing pat-a-cake, holding and feeding the child with a bottle, rocking him while singing, swinging him in a blanket, nibbling his toes, and putting lotion on his skin. The activities also include simple contingency games and power-reversal games that one would normally do with an infant or toddler. For example, the parent makes a squeaky sound each time the child touches the parent's nose (contingency play) or, while sitting on the floor with the child, invites the child to push the parent over on the count of three (power-reversal game).

Research has shown that this form of therapy is highly effective for children suffering from attachment disorders (resulting from abuse, neglect, or separation) and for those who are aggressive, hyperactive, withdrawn, anxious, or depressed (Booth & Jernberg, 2010).

Research on activities with body contact (The importance of touch)

Several studies have demonstrated the physical and psychological benefits of touch. In an interesting experiment, babies who were touched by their mothers during a brief stressful event in a psychology lab showed lower stress levels than babies who were not touched (Tronick, 1995). In another study, school-aged survivors of Hurricane Andrew who were given massage therapy reported less anxiety and depression, as well as lower physiological signs of distress, than those in a control group (Field *et al.*, 1996). Other studies have found that touch can enhance language and social development (Casler, 1965), promote the development of synapses in the brain (Hart, 2008), and improve a child's body image (Weiss, 1990). Even older children can benefit from touch. For example, massage therapy has been shown to reduce aggressive behavior in adolescents (Diego *et al.*, 2002).

In addition to these benefits, nurturing human touch is an essential factor in the development of secure attachment in children (Duhn, 2010). Children who reject human contact (because of previous neglect or abuse) will often accept touch if the therapist or parent incorporates it into simple, playful activities. These games can help restore a child's trust and strengthen attachment (Booth & Jernberg, 2010).

Researchers have begun to understand the neural mechanisms involved in nurturing touch. Positive social interaction, especially if it involves touch, stimulates the production of oxytocin. This, in turn, reduces blood pressure and cortisol levels while stimulating growth and healing (Uvnäs-Moberg & Petersson, 2005).

Research on cooperative games

A specific part of the brain (the orbitofrontal cortex) is activated while playing a game cooperatively but not while playing competitively (Decety *et al.*, 2004). This part of the brain is involved in socially rewarding activities, and it's also the location where decision making and impulse control occur, such as the control of aggressive behavior.

Cooperative games can affect children's behavior in positive ways. Researchers found that active cooperative group games with aggressive children between the ages of three and five years helped reduce aggressive behavior and increase cooperative behavior with their peers (Bay-Hinitz & Wilson, 2005). In another study, active games designed to enhance cooperation and sharing with children showing symptoms of ADHD led to increased cheerfulness, more respect for other children, less aggression, and less anxiety (Garaig-ordobil & Echebarria 1995).

References Cited in Appendix B

Ainsworth, M.D., Bell, S.M., & Stayton, D.J. (1971). Individual differences in strange-situation behavior of one-year-olds. In H.R. Schaffer (Ed.), *The Origins of Human Social Relations*. London & New York: Academic Press.

Astramovich, R.L. (1999). Play therapy theories: a comparison of three approaches. Paper presented at the National Conference of the Association for Counselor Education and Supervision, New Orleans, Louisiana, October 27–31.

Axline, V.M. (1969). *Play Therapy (Revised Edition)*. New York, NY: Ballantine Books.

Bay-Hinitz, A.K. & Wilson, G.R. (2005). A cooperative games intervention for aggressive preschool children. In L.A. Reddy, T.M. Files-Hall, & C.E. Schaefer (Eds.), *Empirically Based Play Interventions for Children* (pp. 169–190). Washington, DC: American Psychological Association.

Bennett M.P. & Lengacher C. (2006a). Humor and laughter may influence health. I. History and background. *Evidence-Based Complementary and Alternative Medicine*, 3(1), 61–63.

Bennett M.P. & Lengacher C. (2006b). Humor and laughter may influence health: II. Complementary therapies and humor in a clinical population. *Evidence-Based Complementary and Alternative Medicine*, 3(2), 187–190.

Bennett M.P. & Lengacher C. (2008). Humor and laughter may influence health: III. Laughter and health outcomes. *Evidence-Based Complementary and Alternative Medicine*, 5(1), 37–40.

Bennett M.P. & Lengacher C. (2009). Humor and laughter may influence health IV: Humor and immune function. *Evidence-Based Complementary and Alternative Medicine*, 6(2), 159–164.

Bettelheim, B. (1987). *A Good Enough Parent: A Book on Child-Rearing.* New York, NY: Alfred A. Knopf, Inc.

Bigelow, A.E., MacLean, K., Proctor, J., Myatt, T., Gillis, R., & Power, M. (2010). Maternal sensitivity throughout infancy: continuity and relation to attachment security. *Infant Behavior and Development*, 33(1), 50–60.

Blend, J. (2009). I got rhythm: music making with children and adolescents. *The International Gestalt Journal*, 32 (2).

Booth, P.B. & Jernberg, A.M. (2010). *Theraplay: Helping Parents and Children Build Better Relationships Through Attachment-Based Play.* San Francisco, CA: Josey-Bass.

Bowlby, J. (1982). *Attachment and Loss. Vol. 1: Attachment* (revised edition). New York, NY: Basic Books.

Bowlby, J. (1988). *A Secure Base: Parent-Child Attachment and Healthy Human Development.* New York, NY: Basic Books.

Brown, S. (2009). *Play: How it Shapes the Brain, Opens the Imagination and Invigorates the Soul.* New York, NY: Avery.

Casler, L. (1965). The study of the effects of extra tactile stimulation on the development of institutionalized infants. *Genetic Psychology Monographs*, 71, 137–175.

Cohen, L.J. (2001). *Playful Parenting.* New York, NY: Ballantine Publishing Group.

DeBenedet, A.T. & Cohen, L.J. (2010). *The Art of Roughhousing: Good Old-Fashioned Horseplay and Why Every Kid Needs It.* Philadelphia, PA: Quirk Books.

Debiec, J. & LeDoux, J.E. (2006). Noradrenergic signaling in the amygdala contributes to the reconsolidation of fear memory: Treatment implications for PTSD. *Annals of the New York Academy of Science*, 1071, 521–524.

Decety, J., Jackson, P.L., Sommerville, J.A., Chaminade, T., & Meltzoff, A.N. (2004). The neural bases of cooperation and competition: an fMRI investigation. *NeuroImage* 23, 744–751.

Diego, M., Field, T., Hernandez-Rief, M., Shaw, J.A., Rothe, E.M., Castellanos, D. & Mesner, L. (2002). Aggressive adolescents benefit from massage therapy. *Adolescence*, 37, 597–607.

Draper, K., Siegel, C., White, J., Solis, C.M., & Mishna, F. (2009). Preschoolers, parents, and teachers (PPT): a preventive intervention with an at risk population. *International Journal of Group Psychotherapy*, 59(2), 221–242.

Duhn, L. (2010). The importance of touch in the development of attachment. *Advanced Neonatal Care*, 10(6), 294–300.

Emerson, W.R. (1989). Psychotherapy with infants and children. *Pre- and Perinatal Psychology Journal*, 3(3), 190–217.

Feldman, P.C., Villanueva, S., Lanne, V., & Devroede, G. (1993). Use of play with clay to treat children with intractable encopresis. *Journal of Pediatrics*, 122(3), 483–488.

Fernandes, S.C. & Arriaga, P. (2010). The effects of clown intervention on worries and emotional responses in children undergoing surgery. *Journal of Health Psychology*, 15(3), 405–415.

Field, T., Seligman, S., Scafidi, F. & Schanberg, S. (1996). Alleviating posttraumatic stress in children following Hurricane Andrew. *Journal of Applied Developmental Psychology*, 17, 37–50.

Field, T., Field, T., Sanders, C., & Nadel, J. (2001). Children with autism display more social behaviors after repeated imitation sessions. *Autism*, 5, 317–323.

Fraiberg, S.H. (1959). *The Magic Years: Understanding and Handling the Problems of Early Childhood*. New York, NY: Charles Scribner's Sons, Inc.

Frankenfield, P.K. (1996). The power of humor and play as nursing interventions for a child with cancer: a case report. *Journal of Pediatric Oncology Nursing*, 13(1), 15–20.

Gaensbauer, R.J. (1995). Trauma in the preverbal period. *Psychoanalytic Study of the Child*, 50, 122–149.

Gaensbauer, R.J. & Siegel, C.H. (1995). Therapeutic approaches to posttraumatic stress disorder in infants and toddlers. *Infant Mental Health Journal*, 16(4), 292–305.

Gallese, V. (2007). Embodied simulation: from mirror neuron systems to interpersonal relations. *Novartis Foundation Symposium*, 278, 3–12.

Garaigordobil, M. & Echebarria, A. (1995). Assessment of a peer-helping program on children's development. *Journal of Research in Childhood Education*, 10, 63–70.

Goodheart, A. (1994). *Laughter Therapy*. Santa Barbara, CA: Less Stress Press.

Greenspan, S.I. & Wieder, S. (1997). Developmental patterns and outcomes in infants and children with disorders in relating and communicating: A chart review of 200 cases of children with autistic spectrum disorders. *Journal of Developmental and Learning Disorders*, 1, 87–141.

Greenspan, S.I. & Wieder, S. (2006). *Engaging Autism: Using the Floortime Approach to Help Children Relate, Communicate, and Think*. Cambridge, MA: Da Capo Press.

Gunsberg, A. (1989). Empowering young abused and neglected children through contingency play. *Childhood Education*, Fall, 8–10.

Hambridge, G. (1982). Structured play therapy. In G. Landreth (Ed.), *Play Therapy: Dynamics of the Process of Counseling With Children*. (pp. 105–119). Springfield, IL: Charles C. Thomas.

Hart, S. (2008). *Brain, Attachment, Personality: An introduction to Neuroaffective Development*. London: Karnac Books.

Heimann, M., Laberg, K.E., & Nordøen, B. (2006). Imitative interaction increases social interest and elicited imitation in non-verbal children with autism. *Infant and Child Development*, 15, 297–309.

Jacob, R.G. & Pelham, W.E. (2005). Behavior Therapy. In B.J. Sabock & V.A. Sabock (Eds.), *Comprehensive Textbook of Psychiatry* (8th ed., pp. 2498–2548). Philadelphia, PA: Lippincott, Williams and Wilkins.

Johnson, M.R. & Kreimer, J.L. (2005). Guided fantasy play for chronically ill children: a critical review. In L.A. Reddy, T.M. Files-Hall, & C.E. Schaefer (Eds.), *Empirically Based Play Interventions for Children* (pp. 105–122). Washington, DC: American Psychological Association.

Johnson, D.B., Pedro-Carroll, J.L., & Demanchick, S.P. (2005). The primary mental health project. In L.A. Reddy, T.M. Files-Hall, & C.E. Schaefer (Eds.), *Empirically Based Play Interventions for Children* (pp. 13–30). Washington, DC: American Psychological Association.

Kaufman, B.N. (1994). *Son Rise: The Miracle Continues*. Tiburon, CA: H.J. Kramer, Inc.

Kot, S. & Tyndall-Lind, A. (2005). Intensive play therapy with child witnesses of domestic violence. In L.A. Reddy, T.M. Files-Hall, & C.E. Schaefer (Eds.), *Empirically Based Play Interventions for Children* (pp. 31–49). Washington, DC: American Psychological Association.

Levy, D. (1938). Release therapy in young children. *Psychiatry*, 1, 387–389.

Li, H.C. & Lopez, V. (2008). Effectiveness and appropriateness of therapeutic play intervention in preparing children for surgery: a randomized controlled trial study. *Journal for Specialists in Pediatric Nursing*, 13(2), 63–73.

Maurer, A. (1967). The game of peek-a-boo. *Diseases of the Nervous System*, 28(2), 118–121.

Meltzoff, A. N. (2002). Imitation as a mechanism of social cognition: origins of empathy, theory of mind, and the representation of action. In U. Goswami (Ed.), *Handbook of Childhood Cognitive Development* (pp. 6–25). Oxford: Blackwell Publishers.

Oaklander, V. (2003). Gestalt Play Therapy. In C.E. Schaefer (Ed.), *Foundations of Play Therapy* (pp. 143–155), Hoboken, NJ: John Wiley & Sons, Inc.

Oaklander, V. (1988). *Windows to Our Children: A Gestalt Therapy Approach to Children and Adolescents*. Gouldsboro, ME: The Gestalt Journal Press.

Oaklander, V. (2007). *Hidden Treasure: A Map to the Child's Inner Self*. London: Karnac Books.

Ostler, T. (2011). "Potential space" in therapy: helping a toddler come to terms with her mother's death. *Zero to Three*, 31(6), 10–14.

Panksepp, J. (2007). Can play diminish ADHD and facilitate the construction of the social brain? *Journal of the Canadian Academy of Child and Adolescent Psychiatry*, 16(2), 57–66.

Pellegrini A.D. & Perlmutter, J.C. (1988). The diagnostic and therapeutic roles of children's rough-and-tumble play. *Journal of Child Health Care*, 16(3), 162–168.

Provence, S. & Lipton, R.C. (1962). *Infants in Institutions*. New York, NY: International Universities Press.

Reddy, L.A., Files-Hall, T.M., & Schaefer, C.E. (2005). *Empirically Based Play Interventions for Children*. Washington, DC: American Psychological Association.

Rochat, P. (2007). Intentional action arises from early reciprocal exchanges. *Acta Psychologica*, 124(1), 8–25.

Rogers, C.R. (1951). *Client-Centered Therapy: Its Current Practice, Implications, and Theory*. Boston, MA: Houghton Mifflin.

Rye, N. (2008). Filial therapy for enhancing relationships in families. *The Journal of Family Health Care*, 18(5), 179–181.

Sanefuji, W. & Ohgami, H. (2011). Imitative behaviors facilitate communicative gaze in children with autism. *Infant Mental Health Journal*, 32(1), 134–142.

Saunders, B.E., Berliner, L., & Hanson, R.F. (Eds.). (2003). *Child Physical and Sexual Abuse: Guidelines for Treatment.* Charleston, SC: National Crime Victims Research and Treatment Center.

Semrud-Klikeman, M. & Glass, K. (2010). The relation of humor and child development: social, adaptive, and emotional aspects. *Journal of Child Neurology*, 25(10), 1248–1260.

Shelby, J.S. & Felix, E.D. (2005). Posttraumatic play therapy: the need for an integrated model of directive and nondirective approaches. In L.A. Reddy, T.M. Files-Hall, & C.E. Schaefer (Eds.), *Empirically Based Play Interventions for Children* (pp. 79–103). Washington, DC: American Psychological Association.

Siegel, D.J. & Hartzell, M. (2003). *Parenting from the Inside Out.* New York, NY: Jeremy P. Tarcher/Putnam.

Sroufe, L.A., Egeland, B., Carlson, E.A., & Collins, W.A. (2005). *The Development of the Person: The Minnesota Study of Risk and Adaptation from Birth to Adulthood.* New York, NY: Guilford Press.

Terr, L. (1983). Play therapy and psychic trauma: a preliminary report. In C.E. Schaefer & K.J. O'Connor (Eds.), *Handbook of Play Therapy.* Hoboken, NJ: John Wiley & Sons.

Terr, L. (1988). What happens to early memories of trauma? A study of twenty children under age five at the time of documented traumatic events. *Journal of the American Academy of Child and Adolescent Psychiatry*, 27, 96–104.

Terr, L. (1992). *Too Scared to Cry: Psychic Trauma in Childhood.* New York, NY: Basic Books.

Tronel, S. & Alberini, C.M. (2007). Persistent disruption of a traumatic memory by postretrieval inactivation of glucocorticoid receptors in the amygdala. *Biological Psychiatry*, 62(1), 33–39.

Tronick, E.Z. (1995). Touch in mother-infant interaction. In T. Field (Ed.), *Touch in Early Development.* Mahwah, NJ: Erlbaum.

Uvnäs-Moberg, K. & Petersson, M. (2005). Oxytocin, a mediator of anti-stress, well-being, social interaction, growth and healing. *Zeitschrift für Psychosomatische Medizin und Psychotherapie*, 51(1), 57–80.

VanFleet, R., Scott, D. & Smith, S.K. (2005). Filial therapy: a critical review. In L.A. Reddy, T.M. Files-Hall, & C.E. Schaefer (Eds.), *Empirically Based Play Interventions for Children* (pp. 241–264). Washington, DC: American Psychological Association.

Webb, P. (2001). Play therapy with traumatized children. In G. Landreth (Ed.), *Innovations in Play Therapy: Issues, Processes, and Special Populations* (pp. 289–302). Philadelphia, PA: Brunner-Routledge.

Weiss, S.J. (1990). Parental touching: correlates of a child's body concept and body sentiment. In K.E. Barnard & T.B. Brazelton (Eds.), *Touch: The Foundation of Experience*. Madison, CT: International Universities Press.

Wilkins, J. & Eisenbrown, A.J. (2009). Humor theories and the physiological benefits of laughter. *Holistic Nursing Practice*, 23(6), 349–354.

Williams, J.H. (2008). Self-other relations in social development and autism: multiple roles for mirror neurons and other brain bases. *Autism Research*, 2, 73–90.

Recommended Books for Parents

Aldort, Naomi. (2006). *Raising Our Children, Raising Ourselves*. Bothell, WA: Book Publishers Network.

Armstrong, Thomas. (2000). *In Their Own Way: Discovering and Encouraging Your Child's Multiple Intelligences*. New York, NY: Jeremy P. Tarcher/Putnam.

Aron, Elaine. (2002). *The Highly Sensitive Child: Helping Our Children Thrive When the World Overwhelms Them*. New York, NY: Broadway Books.

Breeding, John. (2007). *The Wildest Colts Make the Best Horses: Defending the Development of Spirited Young People*. United Kingdom: Chipmunkapublishing.

Cohen, Lawrence. (2001). *Playful Parenting*. New York, NY: Ballantine Books.

DeBenedet, Anthony & Lawrence Cohen. (2010). *The Art of Roughhousing: Good Old-Fashioned Horseplay and Why Every Kid Needs it*. Philadelphia, PA: Quirk Books.

Faber, Adele & Elaine Mazlish. (2012). *How to Talk so Kids Will Listen and Listen so Kids Will Talk*. New York, NY: Scribner.

Gordon, Thomas. (2000). *Parent Effectiveness Training: The Proven Program for Raising Responsible Children*. New York, NY: Three Rivers Press.

Holt, John. *How Children Learn*. (1995). New York, NY: Da Capo Press.

Kohn, Alfie. (2005). *Unconditional Parenting: Moving From Rewards and Punishments to Love and Reason*. New York, NY: Atria Books.

Leo, Pam. (2007). *Connection Parenting: Parenting through Connection instead of Coercion, through Love instead of Fear (2nd edition)*. Deadwood, OR: Wyatt-MacKenzie Publishing.

Luvmour, Sambhava & Josette Luvmour. (2007). *Everyone Wins: Cooperative Games and Activities.* Gabriola Island, B.C., Canada: New Society Publishers.

Miles, Karen. (2006). *Psychology Today: The Power of Loving Discipline.* Indianapolis, IN: Alpha Books.

O'Mara, Peggy. (2000). *Natural Family Living: The Mothering Magazine Guide to Parenting.* New York, NY: Pocket Books.

Orlick, Terry. (2006). *Cooperative Games and Sports: Joyful Alternatives for Everyone.* Champaign, IL: Human Kinetics.

Rosenberg, Marshall. (2005). *Raising Children Compassionately: Parenting the Nonviolent Communication Way.* Encinitas, CA: Puddle Dancer Press.

Samalin, Nancy & Martha M. Jablow. (1998). *Loving Your Child is not Enough: Positive Discipline That Works.* New York. NY: Penguin.

Siegel, Daniel J. & Mary Hartzell. (2003). *Parenting from the Inside Out.* New York, NY: Jeremy P. Tarcher/Putnam.

Solter, Aletha. (1989). *Helping Young Children Flourish.* Goleta, CA: Shining Star Press.

Solter, Aletha. (1998). *Tears and Tantrums: What to Do When Babies and Children Cry.* Goleta, CA: Shining Star Press.

Solter, Aletha. (2001). *The Aware Baby* (revised edition). Goleta, CA: Shining Star Press.

Solter, Aletha. (2006). *Raising Drug-Free Kids: 100 Tips for Parents.* New York, NY: Da Capo Press.

About the Author

ALETHA SOLTER, PH.D., is a Swiss/American developmental psychologist, workshop leader, and consultant. She studied with Dr. Jean Piaget at the University of Geneva, Switzerland, where she earned a Master's Degree in human biology. She holds a Ph.D. in psychology from the University of California, Santa Barbara. Her four previous books have been translated into many languages. The titles are: *The Aware Baby*, *Helping Young Children Flourish*, *Tears and Tantrums*, and *Raising Drug-Free Kids*. She has also written original research articles as well as numerous articles for parents.

Dr. Solter has led workshops in 16 countries and is recognized internationally as an expert on attachment, trauma, and non-punitive discipline. She founded the Aware Parenting Institute in 1990 to help promote the approach described in her books. There is a growing list of certified Aware Parenting instructors who are helping to spread this information around the world.

If you would like to schedule a consultation or organize a workshop, please contact her at the address below.

The Aware Parenting Institute
Post Office Box 206
Goleta, California 93116
U.S.A.

Phone & Fax: (805) 968–1868
Email: solter@awareparenting.com
Website: www.awareparenting.com

What Is Aware Parenting?

AWARE PARENTING IS a philosophy of child rearing that is based on research in child development. It questions most traditional assumptions about children and proposes a new approach that can significantly improve relationships within a family. Parents who follow this approach raise children who are cooperative, compassionate, competent, nonviolent, and drug free.

The philosophy is described in Dr. Aletha Solter's books. Please see the Aware Parenting Institute website for more information (www.awareparenting.com).

Aware Parenting consists of the following three elements:

Attachment-style parenting
- Natural childbirth and early bonding
- Plenty of physical contact
- Prolonged breast-feeding
- Prompt responsiveness to crying
- Sensitive attunement

Non-punitive discipline
- No punishments of any kind (including spanking, time-out, and artificial consequences)
- No rewards or bribes
- A search for underlying needs and feelings
- Anger management for parents
- Peaceful conflict-resolution (family meetings, mediation, etc.)

Healing from stress and trauma
- Recognition of stress and trauma as primary causes of behavioral and emotional problems
- Emphasis on prevention of stress and trauma
- Recognition of the healing effects of play, laughter, and crying in the context of a loving parent-child relationship
- Respectful, empathic listening and acceptance of children's emotions